"Marriage books written by people who aren't therapists or marriage researchers are usually full of 'common nonsense' that has little bearing upon marital success. *Choosing Us* is the exception. It is the long-awaited resource for couples committed to building progressive, equitable relationships where both partners have highly demanding careers. It is not a how-to guide to replicating Gail and Brian's relationship. It is a source of wisdom for creating your own."

—**Chanequa Walker-Barnes**, clinical psychologist and author of *I Bring the Voices of My People*

"How can we flourish together? What does mutual submission really entail? Why must I look inward before casting blame on my partner? When there are no models, how do we build something healthy together? While there are countless marriage books, few focus on cultivating egalitarian unions where couples grow together and individually fulfill their created purpose. *Choosing Us* achieves this and equips readers to love selflessly, even when it's counterintuitive and inconvenient. This book will bless your marriage and empower you to love your partner more authentically. It illuminates how couples can thrive beyond the honeymoon phase and go the distance together."

—**Dominique DuBois Gilliard**, author of *Subversive Witness: Scripture's Call to Leverage Privilege* and *Rethinking Incarceration: Advocating for Justice That Restores*

"Marriage is a journey, and no matter where you and your spouse are in it, *Choosing Us* is an important guide. The Bantums share with tender honesty, inviting us into their past, and offer incisive questions, encouraging us in our present. They do not shy away from pointing out how gender, racial, and ethnic identity and cultural norms can shape faith and marriage, inviting all readers to consider the assumptions and expectations we bring into it. Do yourself and your marriage a favor. Read this book."

—**Kathy Khang**, author of *Raise Your Voice: Why We Stay Silent and How to Speak Up*

"*Choosing Us* arrived on my desk at the right moment in my marriage of thirty years. Without minimizing how hard it is to sustain a marriage, especially when negotiating differences in race and culture, the Bantums demonstrate that marriage is difficult but worth it. They open the inner sanctum of their trials and growth as a couple struggling to fight their own demons and those inherited from family and culture, letting the light in and the wisdom born out of their faith and struggle to come through. *Choosing Us* speaks transparently to readers of our naive assumptions about love and lopsided gender roles that we bring into marriage. Gail and Brian bring their full selves to this book, two strong-minded people willing to listen, negotiate, forgive, and grow. *Choosing Us* offers readers invaluable lessons on how to use natural differences and conflicts to work toward a loving relationship that is built on the strength of one's differences, creating a healthy marriage as the first step in building a just world."

—**Renita J. Weems**, minister, biblical scholar, and author of *What Matters Most: Ten Passionate Lessons on the Song of Solomon*

Choosing US

Choosing US

Marriage and
Mutual Flourishing
in a World of
Difference

Gail Song Bantum and Brian Bantum

BrazosPress

a division of Baker Publishing Group
Grand Rapids, Michigan

© 2022 by Gail Song Bantum and Brian Bantum

Published by Brazos Press
a division of Baker Publishing Group
PO Box 6287, Grand Rapids, MI 49516-6287
www.brazospress.com

Printed in the United States of America

Library of Congress Cataloging-in-Publication Data
Names: Bantum, Gail Song, 1975– author. | Bantum, Brian, 1975– author.
Title: Choosing us : marriage and mutual flourishing in a world of difference / Gail
    Song Bantum and Brian Bantum.
Description: Grand Rapids, Michigan : Brazos Press, a division of Baker Publishing
    Group, [2022]
Identifiers: LCCN 2021033317 | ISBN 9781587435379 (cloth) | ISBN 9781493435227
    (ebook) | ISBN 9781493435234 (pdf)
Subjects: LCSH: Interracial marriage—Religious aspects—Christianity.
Classification: LCC BT707.3 .B36 2022 | DDC 261.8/358—dc23
LC record available at https://lccn.loc.gov/2021033317

Scripture quotations are from the New Revised Standard Version of the Bible, copyright © 1989 National Council of the Churches of Christ in the United States of America. Used by permission. All rights reserved.

Baker Publishing Group publications use paper produced from sustainable forestry practices and post-consumer waste whenever possible.

22 23 24 25 26 27 28   7 6 5 4 3 2 1

To our Regroup squad:

Beth and Justin
Carrie and Jeff
Michelle and Jeremy
Liz and Kevin
Kenneth (and Kathleen)
Marshaé (and Liz)

for the gift of letting us
journey with you

Contents

Prologue

Our Why

In some ways, our marriage and relationship has had a certain storybook feel. Two young college students, at schools three hundred miles apart, are introduced by Jeannette, a mutual friend. A first letter. A first call that lasts two and a half hours. She calls him back, and they talk for another two and a half hours. More letters. More long-distance calls (between 11 p.m. and 5 a.m., when it's ten cents a minute). They fall in love. *Then* they meet in person. They share a first awkward car ride, neither of them looking at the other because voices were all they knew. A year later, he proposes. Another year later, they're married. It's practically a movie.

But a lot can happen in twenty-seven years. A mutual friend of ours set me (Gail) up with Brian because she had heard that my mom had just died and knew that his dad had recently died as well. Unexpectedly, a serious long-distance relationship emerged. But when I told my dad I wanted to marry Brian, I was confronted with a heartbreaking choice: either obey him

1

and not marry Brian because he was a Black man, or disobey my dad and potentially lose years of relationship with him. He asked me to leave the house when I chose Brian. As a result, I had to navigate life in close quarters with Brian's family for every school break thereafter. We decided to get married while we were still in college, grieving the fact that my dad wouldn't be at our wedding. Upon graduating, we quickly had to figure out how to pursue each of our calls to ministry. A year later, we were figuring out life with a newborn while Brian headed back to school for seminary. Two years later, we had our second child and grieved the loss of Brian's mom to cancer. As if those losses weren't enough, during those years we also endured three miscarriages.

But in fits and starts we made our way. Brian graduated from seminary as I scrappily worked part time, then full time, as a worship minister. We were unexpectedly pregnant with our third child, trying desperately to figure out how to raise three young kids while completing school and pursuing our vocations. Eventually, and years later, I would heed the call to seminary while Brian pursued his doctorate. Both of us still working on the side, the baby tagged along with us to classes, lectures, and music practices like a boss! A few years later, we moved to Seattle, where Brian landed his first job in the field he had worked so hard for, while my gifts would also be fully received and realized in this new season. My dad and I were finally able to reconcile twenty-one years later as I heard him earnestly say to me, "Brian is a good man." While pointing to a Korean-Black, mixed pop artist on the television, a woman named Insooni, he also said, "She's my favorite artist. If you'd had a daughter, I bet she would've looked like her." Tears! That's my Korean father's way of saying, "I'm sorry." He died one year later, in 2017, after battling cancer.

This journey was anything but a straight line for us. We both had a sense of call. We both wanted kids. But what that looked like, when to have kids, who would work, who would stay home, how to balance it all, and how to build a life together was a work in progress. Without a plan, our home life fell into the common tropes: Gail at home with the kids, me at school. I (Brian) got into Duke for a master's program. It seemed easier (to me) to keep picking up side jobs to make ends meet, but this also meant more hours of Gail at home with little ones. Sometimes it meant tense conversations because Gail's dream was drifting further away while I was on a path toward mine. And sometimes it was hard for me to hear, if I heard at all, because I felt like I was working all the time. I was reading just enough, or maybe just a few pages, and felt like I wasn't measuring up. The journey involved watching as Gail got passed over at our church because she's a woman. It was years and years of taking turns while other people seemed to be on a fast track or enjoying their twenties while we plodded along, just trying to get through. It included watching as my (Brian's) mother endured and ultimately died from lung cancer.

As we raised our kids, questions of race and ethnicity and belonging continued to press. How do we instill in them a sense of being Korean? Of being Black? Of navigating racial ambiguity and not quite fitting in? And in the midst of it all, it was discovering ways to love and be present for each other, trying to create a new culture in our life together. Along the way, we've come to realize that everything goes in the pot, so to speak. Being committed to each other's flourishing in a world of racism and sexism means we need each other to become our whole selves.

Now we've begun to reflect on our journey more intentionally, as well as the journey we've shared with other couples trying to find their way in a world of difference. This book has been tugging at us for a few years. Having been married for twenty-five years, working as a pastor (Gail) and a professor (Brian), we've walked with many couples who are asking questions about marriage, balancing careers, and navigating race in a world where the violence of white supremacy only increases.

When we got married at twenty-one in a little church in Maryland, there was nothing elaborate—a church that neither of us were members of, a small reception at Brian's mom's house with his family, a few of Brian's church folk, some random neighbors, and a handful of Gail's friends. We had no idea what we were in for or where we were going. We had talked about going into ministry together, about *maybe* planting a church, but we were certain that whatever we did, we would be in it together. Those senses of call took us on some winding paths. For me (Gail), it started as a part-time music director, then volunteer choir director, then worship leader, then seminarian, to associate pastor to executive pastor to lead pastor. The path for me (Brian) was just as circuitous: high school history teacher, educational specialist, seminarian, full-time TA and any other part-time job I could muster, doctoral student, then professor.

It's easy to imagine that where we are now was the plan all along, but in actuality, it's all been about listening and making mistakes, then trying to listen some more. There was never a plan, only an intention to do whatever we could together, to make room for the other, and to avoid some of the pain we experienced in our own homes growing up. While we did not end up planting a church together or working together in ministry, our work and vocations dovetail. We still work out of a deep sense of call to the church and to serve as witnesses to God's presence and work in the world. But we have also found our own unique ways of living into those calls, and it was only together that we actually found how those calls rang most truly in each of us.

In the midst of creating a home and family together, we were also navigating realities of gender and race. As a Korean

American woman and a Black, mixed man, we were both learning ourselves and the way legacies of race and patriarchy had shaped our world. We do our work in a world where our bodies matter, where we are created to enjoy and be enjoyed, and yet the fallenness and pain of this world afflict us in real, concrete ways. What does it mean to be a couple, to be for one another in this kind of world? This has been our question and our journey. It's what we teach, preach, and try to live every day. Along the way, we have been surprised to see how some of our mistakes and forging through the bush have resonated with people we've walked with and taught. What we offer isn't necessarily the wisdom of experts but simply the journey of two people who have been wandering these woods called marriage for a good bit of time.

Little did we know that an idea for a book would mean writing it in the midst of a pandemic, confined to work and live in the same space for a year. We could not have imagined the sudden shift from being on the verge of living as empty nesters to living in a full house of five people again. (And of course, *this* was the time to get a puppy.) In many ways it has been a gift to be together. But being confined to life with one another, trying to live and work in the same space with the same people all day, every day, as many of us have had to learn, can also accentuate fissures, pull up long-buried tensions, and remind us of difficult questions we sometimes avoid about ourselves and the people we live with.

Early on in the writing process, we took a walk to discuss the project and ideas for chapters. It began excitedly. *We are actually doing this! Writing a book together!* But soon, uneven silences crept in, frustrated responses bubbled up, and clarifying questions (laced with the residue of past arguments) finally spilled over, until I (Brian) blurted out, "I don't work for you! I'm not on your staff!" The rest of the walk home was filled with awkward silence.

Worn down, tired because of our new puppy, and our working rhythms undone, little silences became little snips that would take a few days to smooth out. In truth, we haven't fought more than we did while writing this book.

The frustrations were never about one individual thing. They were about trying to navigate expectations, opportunities, and the oftentimes unspoken dance of trying to support the other person while also pursuing what each of us is called to do. As with most marriages, it's the same argument over and over, just in different keys.

Eventually, we found some patterns that worked (apparently puppies need a lot of time in their crates). Slowly, we found our way to an equilibrium, like we always have.

Neither of us comes from ideal, stable families. We didn't know what a healthy marriage looked like. When we met at nineteen, we had very different ideas of what marriage was, when was an ideal time to marry, and what we thought our lives would look like in twenty years. By the time we were twenty, we couldn't imagine life without each other. By twenty-one, we were married. And we were making it all up as we went along. There were no married couples in our lives to ask us probing questions or for us to pattern our lives after. There were certainly no interracial couples who could help us sort out our racial journeys and histories or how they were shaping our newly formed family. And in our evangelical and Pentecostal churches, there was no pattern for two people with gifts and callings where the woman didn't have to put her calling aside for the sake of the family.

So we started with some simple questions. What were things from our childhood that we most wanted to avoid? Where were the patterns of violence or distrust that we wanted to end with us? In this time, we also arrived at our golden rule: We don't do anything big until we both feel total peace in the decision (more about that in chap. 6).

But everything else was trial and error, trust and commitment to being for the other, and more trial, and more error. We had to navigate difficult questions of race in the Korean community. We had to mine formations of masculinity. We had to figure out questions of life together as settled answers got tossed around with each new child or new city or new vocational opportunity or shift. And here we are, twenty-plus years later, still learning, still growing.

While we share a lot of our own story here, this book also reflects our experience of mentoring many couples over the years whose stories are similar to ours. Many of these couples were looking for a different model of marriage than one in which the man intentionally or unintentionally "leads" the family. Others were interracial, while still others had less than ideal family histories. We've wanted to offer not *the* way marriages or relationships ought to be; rather we've offered *a* way—a way that opens up possibilities for both people to discover what flourishing might look like for them and what flourishing life together might offer to the world.

We say "*a* way" because we are sure we have made mistakes. We have done the best we could with what we had. But the possibilities we imagined and the options we refused also grew out of our unique stories. As an interracial couple, we are aware that our life can't always be reproduced in our mentees, students, or children. Traditions and legacies are gifts that are offered so that our children might create their own traditions. We only hope they see the people and the histories that shaped us and how those stories continue to live in them.

Similarly, couples we walk with carry their own histories, scars, joys, and ways of navigating the world. A marriage is not a sourdough recipe that can be perfected with just enough time. Part of our joy is watching our mentees, students, and children create new ways of living, loving, and creating community in their midst in ways we could not have imagined.

We offer our story and hope you can find something of your-self in it. And whether there are places of resonance or difference, we hope this book sparks a conversation about who you are, who the person you're with is, and what you are creating together. Whether you are an interracial couple, or a couple with shared racial and ethnic stories, or a couple within the LGBTQ+ community, your story is not ours, and our story is not the totality of all marriages or relationships. Rather, we hope this book can be an invitation to discover your own story.

We are also aware that a book on marriage and relationships can be difficult in the midst of relationships that are struggling through pain. Too many marriages are spaces of violence, manipulation, and abuse. As you read these pages, hear us in saying that the calls to covenant and to commitment are calls that assume reciprocity and love as the basic shape of marital life. Violence, abuse, and manipulation are acts of dehumanization and violations of covenantal commitments, and God wants more than that for all of us.

We also want to offer a quick note on sex. If you bought this book and began eagerly looking for the chapter on sexual intimacy, you may be disappointed. It may seem unusual to have a book on marriage and relationships and not talk about sex. But marriage is more than who you have sex with. We also recognize that how couples think about sex and sexual intimacy is unique to each couple and tied to the ways they were formed, including experiences of violence and abuse, harmful associations of sex with shame, and the many, varied ways couples can enjoy each other.

While we both believe that the greatest intimacy and power of sex comes in monogamous, covenanted relationships, we also know that just because sex happens in those relationships doesn't mean that the act is holy or beautiful or mutual. We also acknowledge that people have sex outside the confines of marriage. When it comes down to it, vows and a ceremony are not what make the act holy or unholy. Sex is a beautiful aspect of being human and an expression of what it means to enjoy and be enjoyed, one way of seeing and feeling what it means to experience joy and ecstasy.

In a real way, sex is an aspect of the relating that we'll describe throughout this book. Sex is an act of mutual listening, a desire for the other to experience bliss and joy in trust that your partner wants the same for you. Sex in a covenanted relationship is discovering the depths of this one person and sometimes going through seasons that seem slow, dry, or mundane but never resting in those deserts. It is the discovery of new ways of enjoying and the recognition of how new seasons of life invigorate the intimacy of sharing your body with the other. Whether this looks like sex all the time in all kinds of places or sex in regular, scheduled intervals or sex on seemingly rare occasions, it is never simply release or consumption. Rather, it is an act that lives and expresses your journey together, and that requires discovery of yourself, learning the other, a willingness to grow and adapt, trust in the other, and patience.

We hope that not only couples will read this book but also anyone who is hoping for a sojourner in navigating the world shaped by ideas of race and gender and sexuality that have boxed us in and seemed to determine who to be with, and how to be with them, in this world.

Marriage is not an institution separate from race and gender. When people get married, questions of masculinity and femininity and of race and racism don't vanish. Marriage has historically been a way for ideas about gender and race to be turned into mechanisms of control and exclusion. There is a reason marriage was forbidden for slaves, that interracial marriage was illegal until 1967, and that same-sex marriage was illegal in many states until 2015. Marriage has been an arena in which some of the most violent and pernicious legacies of racism and sexism persist and are reproduced.

But when we begin to see marriage not as the pinnacle of what it means to be made in the image of God but as just one good relationship of many, we can also begin to see how marriage is connected to dynamics of friendship, sex, gender, race, mundane everydayness, and life-changing transformations. In marriage, all of these dynamics coalesce into a difficult and beautiful creation—a new culture forged in the life of two people joined together. That new creation reverberates beyond those two people, whether it's in their vocation, in the people they mentor or serve, in what they create or build, or in the children they raise.

We've seen the harm wrought by rigid ideas of marriage. We have also seen the ways that this life together can be a space of fullness and purpose and joy. But it might not be everything we'd dreamed it would be (#relationshipgoals #powercouple). It might require spaces of uncertainty, of patience, of one person going slow so the other can go fast and trusting it won't always be that way. It will be seasons of uncertainty where our manna is the other person's wins while we plod along. But part of what makes life together powerful is that it never requires one person alone to sacrifice, to slow down, to wither. If a couple is to flourish, both people will need opportunities to live into their gifts.

And in the end, it might be discovering that flourishing is something quite different from what we had imagined at the beginning. To live into this, we have had to ask questions about how our bodies do work in the world. We've had to become students of one another, even when it feels like the tests keep changing. We've had to take steps back and ask what hasn't been working and trust that the other person wants to find out too. The story keeps unfolding.

This is our story—the story of a Korean American woman and a Black, mixed man trying to discover what it means to make a life together. To become *we*.

ONE

The Plan

People change. Maybe you should give this some time to figure out who you are before you get married," she said. We had flown to California for me (Gail) to introduce Brian to a few of my aunts and extended family. Sitting in the dining room with them, Brian and I tried to listen as best we could. They clearly loved us and wanted the best for us. Brian and I were in love, and after ten months of dating and thousands of dollars spent on phone calls, stamps, and plane and bus tickets, we knew we wanted to spend the rest of our lives together.

We were also twenty years old, and a young twenty at that. My aunts knew that we would change over time, and they were worried for us.

We replied, "Yes, we are going to change. But we are going to grow toward each other." We were *so* smart. Of course we were going to change, we thought to ourselves. We even knew how we were going to change. We had a plan for our lives, a calling even.

Now, with our own children nearly grown, we see what they saw. We had no idea what was in store for us or who we were.

But part of what changed us wasn't just graduating from college or the first job or clarifying vocational goals. Our life together was a journey of discovering the questions we didn't realize we were asking, the histories and the stories that kept pulling and tugging and shaping us under the surface of our lives.

While we weren't wrong to believe we'd grow toward one another, there was a fundamental misconception: we thought we knew who we were to begin with. In our young minds and hearts, we looked at one another and thought growing toward one another was simply a matter of loving the other person. But we didn't understand that we were trees that had been planted in very different orchards and nurtured in different soils. Just as a tree has little understanding of itself as it grows, we had so much to learn about ourselves and our own stories, even while we were trying to grow toward this new person in our lives.

Self-discovery is an ongoing process because we are never finished becoming. As each year passes, as we enter into periods of lack or plenty, hardship or joy, and loss or abundance, the light of who we are refracts a little differently in new moments. The growth we experienced in ourselves and toward one another was sometimes a series of conscious decisions and explicit conversations. At other times, the growth was stopping and breathing for a moment, taking stock of what was underneath the frustration or the boredom or the work of just getting through each day, to ask ourselves who we were and who we were becoming, for ourselves and for the other person, in that moment.

As we begin to think about relationships, even before we can begin to talk about what it means to join our lives together, we need to first ask who we think we are. There are plenty of personality types and gift assessments and premarital work-shops on family systems, but part of the question of knowing ourselves is beginning to recognize that we cannot know the totality of who we are in that moment or who we are going to be. And yet, in the midst of this unknowing, there are tributaries and rivers and lakes of history, dynamics of power and oppression, formations of masculinity and femininity, structures of race and ethnic identity, all working in the midst of the stream that is our life.

The work of charting the rivers of history that live in us and have shaped us never ends. Learners of a way, be it an instrument or a life of faith or an art, are always learning and discovering something new about themselves and how they've changed over the years. This is no less true of ourselves as individuals. But when we bind our lives to another and live in daily intimacy and closeness, these transformations are even more pronounced.

When two people choose to become a "we," they begin to discover more of who each person is. In our own experience, and in counseling couples navigating relationships, preparing for marriage, or working through years of marriage, we have seen how the illusion of certainty and assumptions become this extra baggage that fills the rooms of their lives until they have no room to move or to even see the other person. But the biggest assumptions that rarely emerge in these conversations are the ones people make about themselves. Usually, people think they know themselves. That's why they can be so sure they are right and the other person is wrong. Not only do they know themselves, but they also know their own history, the way they are navigating their community, and the questions or discomfort of being different.

This certainty might be about issues of character or personality traits. But maybe they haven't asked how, as a Black man, for example, they have navigated predominately white spaces and how that experience has shaped or is shaping them. Maybe as a man, they haven't asked how dynamics of gender are moving under the surface of the frustrations at home and the ease they feel at work. Even while we are discovering who we are, we are also navigating a world shaped by race, gender, and sexuality. And none of these are realities that we fully understand in ourselves at any given time.

We want to begin this book by reflecting on personhood. We are being intentional in avoiding the word "individual," because no one exists apart from communities and families and stories. A person is always a patchwork. But a person is also a point where all of those stories and people and communities coalesce into one beautiful, unique burst of light. What happens when two bursts of light join?

To understand this, we need to think about the ones who are being joined.

We Both Had Plans

As teenagers, each of us had a plan for our lives, of who we thought we were and how we thought our lives would go. Here were our respective plans:

Gail's Plan	*Brian's Plan*
• Become the first Asian American female conductor of the New York Philharmonic • Produce albums on the side for artists like Mary J. Blige, in my "free time" • Live in a cute condo in NYC • *Consider* getting married when I turn thirty • Marry an athlete • No kids • Livin' the life!	• Get married • Have three to four kids • Become a pastor or a teacher • Coach soccer • Live in my hometown near my mom

Clearly, we were a match made in heaven! And plans change. We lose people we love. Small and not-so-small knocks change the trajectory of our lives, and sometimes we wake up realizing the life we had imagined for ourselves did not materialize. But we also can't quite imagine wanting a life that could have been either.

For us those losses and those meetings all seemed to ping "just so," bringing us together during our sophomore year of college. And that meeting would wreck our plans, at least in the ways we had imagined them.

Gail

My plans were upended when my mother suddenly died of cancer after my first year of college. I met Brian through a mutual friend not too long after I returned to school. He was an athlete, but a nerdy one. I started to reconsider my calling in life. We married while we were both still in college. At age twenty-one, I decided to enter vocational ministry and got a job as a musical worship leader. By age twenty-three, we had our first child, and six years later, we had two more. At age thirty-one, I entered seminary with three kids in tow between the ages of two and seven.

I'm a pastor. He's a professor. And I think: *I've become my mother.*

There is always more to the story than lists. In reality, I've always been told that I have big dreams, sometimes seemingly impossible dreams. My dad made me learn the violin from the time I was three years old, which later evolved into learning many instruments toward the goal of becoming a conductor. Looking back, I'm not sure I ever knew a life apart from learning, honing, crafting, and perfecting something with the intensity they say being a professional musician or athlete cultivates. Music was what I gave my life to—hours upon hours nearly every day—working to get into one of the few elite music conservatories in the world. By the time I started my senior year of high school, I had already participated in major summer music festivals and received acceptance letters from The Juilliard School in New York City and the Eastman School of Music in Rochester. I'm sure there was a bit of talent mixed in with the hard work to get to where I was, but I valued my determination and laser focus more than anything. I had a plan. And everything was coming together just as I had planned, or so I thought.

Two years later, I found myself home after my first year of college on summer break, caring for my mother. She had been diagnosed with stage four lung cancer out of the blue. After she fought for life for over seven weeks, my brother and I sat with her in the hospital room as she labored for her final breath. Those weeks simultaneously felt like forever and not enough. That summer changed everything.

Death, sudden loss, and suffering shift perspective. My mother's death, and pondering a life that seemed too short, made "my plan" seem ridiculous. I found myself questioning everything. My mom wanted to be a pastor, struggled through seminary at age forty with English as a second language, and was barely able to see it through to fruition before she died. "Who cares if I became the first this or the first that if I could literally die tomorrow. What am I doing with my life?" I asked myself.

It was one month after she died that I had my first conversation with Brian over the phone. It was only about six months after she died that I sensed a strong and unrelenting call to ministry—a vision and a remembrance of a prophetic word I'd received when I was eight years old at my parents' Pentecostal church in Chicago.

I believe God used that time, when my heart was especially tender, attentive, and desperate, to speak truths into my life and to remind me of the promise spoken over me years prior. They were truths about my vocation and the people I would need to thrive, whether I realized it or not. At the time, Brian was not like *anything* I had imagined in a partner. He had dreams of being a suburban dad with four children (four!) living the cul-de-sac life. He liked music I had never really heard of. When I first talked to him, the only reference I had of how he might be was Carlton from *The Fresh Prince of Bel-Air*. In the end, I didn't imagine having kids initially and wanted to live a career-driven life in New York City, the city where my parents had immigrated. None of what Brian represented and wanted was in my plan.

Brian

Reading Gail's account of how her life plans changed, I am reminded of just how little I had to give up. For me, the risk was hoping for something more, not letting go of big dreams.

My plans before meeting Gail were pretty ordinary: to marry, have kids, have a steady job as a teacher or coach, and live in the suburbs near my mom. But everything changed one night my sophomore year of college. A mutual friend told me about Gail. "She loves soccer," she said. Apparently, that was enough. I learned that Gail went to music school and that her mom had recently passed away from cancer (my dad had died the previous year too). In hindsight, I'm not sure what I was thinking. I am sure that it came off a little strange and desperate when I wrote her a letter introducing myself. Then I called her, before the letter had even arrived.

I was just hoping to make a good impression, but we talked for two and a half hours, then hung up, and she called me back, and we talked for two and a half more hours. That's how it started.

I don't think I would call it "love at first hearing" or say that I knew this was the person I was going to marry. But I knew there was something there, even if I couldn't describe what. When I picked up the phone, I didn't know I'd find someone to navigate this in-between life with. I didn't know my understanding of Scripture or theology or life would get flipped inside out. I didn't know I could be so afraid of losing someone. I didn't know I'd be a person who would write books or even expect to be listened to. But in the hours of conversations, the heated conversations about women in ministry or the Bible, in laughing and writing letters, my plans were not so much being thrown out but hollowed out and filled in with a richer and more expansive vision. I had plans to be a pastor of a Southern Baptist church, the "head of the household," and a teacher in a Christian high school. But the containers I had been given were too small for the world that I met in Gail. With each of our conversations, the world I knew was being poured out to make space for a bigger world.

In some ways the plans weren't too far off. In other ways, today I am living a life I could not have dreamed of—as a pastor's spouse, a professor, and a father of three amazing boys. But it was completely unexpected and seemed beyond the realm of possibility. Some of the impossibility was just in the narrow world I lived within, theologically and socially. Part of it was realizing that I was incredibly change-averse (and still am). And part of it was just the fact that Gail is someone I would have never had the courage to meet in person. I would have noticed her and probably had a crush from a distance. To be honest, when I first started talking with her, I thought she was "Blacker" than me, which struck me as odd since she is Korean. And I didn't know what I thought about that, about meeting this Asian American woman who seemed to have a soulful way about her. Truthfully, though, it was my own blackness and disconnection from Black life that I saw in her and that created questions in me. And that was all going to be part of the journey, a journey that began with a phone call.

Embracing Change

When we first met, I (Brian) cautiously smelled my food before I ate it. I turned up my nose at sushi, ginger, and Japanese curry. But one day, I ordered a tuna sandwich, not realizing that it was raw. And to my amazement, I liked it. Loved it actually. That was my gateway to sushi. But I drew the line at ginger. Then I tried a bit again eight years later, only to find that I also loved it. Food is one small way that I came to realize that who I am is always changing. And these new things that I was encountering were also opening up places for us to eat, foods we could order together, creating new possibilities and new connections.

It feels like something you'd read in a Hallmark card, but it's true: everyone changes. Everything changed for us the day we first spoke on the phone, even if we didn't realize it at the time. We took a step onto a new road, with no map other than a sense that where we'd been in life wasn't where we wanted to go.

It hasn't been easy. There have been moments and periods of time when we wondered if the marriage would last or if we could endure lying next to someone from whom we felt painfully distant—a pain that could only come from tearing. We've had to figure out who we are, as individuals and as a "we," and how our individual stories shape our shared everyday life. Life together has been both a settling and a stirring. Whether asking questions about who God is and who God called us to be, or navigating the racial and ethnic communities that we felt both connected to and distant from, we've had to ask ourselves who we were in the midst of these shifts and discoveries and who we would be to each other. We continually find ourselves, only to find that we've become something new as well—and that we have to learn each other all over again with each new bend in the road.

But in the midst of this, we had no models, no people to journey with or other families that we really saw ourselves in, especially who we were becoming together. In truth, we were *so* different. While we connected quickly, it was clear early on that our plans were very different, as were our stories, our likes and dislikes, and our formations.

I (Gail) am a Korean American whose faith was deeply formed in Black and Korean Pentecostal traditions. I love R&B, soul, and Brazilian music and was shaped in predominantly Korean and Black cultures, and ultimately saw myself living single in New York City.

I (Brian) came to Christ in a Southern Baptist church, didn't believe women could be in ministry, liked alternative rock and country music (it's a long story), grew up in predominantly white spaces with my white family, and hoped to eventually live in a nice little house in suburban Maryland with a wife and four kids.

These differences never defined us, and by the time we met we were already undergoing all the changes that young adulthood brings. But initially these differences were reminders that in every situation we had very different frames of reference for how to think about what to do on a Saturday, or where to eat, or what to work toward. It wasn't always the specific differences that mattered but recognizing that there were differences that needed to be discovered.

In varied ways, those early senses of call and vocation never left us. I (Gail) shifted from classical music performance and dreams of conducting orchestras to leading worship, leading leaders, and eventually leading a church. I was conducting in ways I could not have imagined as the dream manifested in unexpected ways. I (Brian) had thought about ministry but was always drawn to teaching and coaching. I only had a vague sense of what professors did. My only strong models of a teacher were my high school history teacher and soccer coach. Twenty years later, I find myself teaching in seminary and "coaching" doctoral students.

We had dreams and calls and hopes, but we also had few models of what it looked like to get there. And when we began our life together, those dreams shifted and expanded and twisted along the way. In the midst of what we knew, and especially everything we didn't know, the path was hard and beautiful and surprising.

Stretch Marks

What happens when one or both people in a marriage begin to change? It's rare that we feel the change and say to ourselves, "This is amazing! Look how much I'm growing!" More often, unexpected circumstances lay things bare in our lives, showing us something about ourselves that we didn't know was there or that we thought we had dealt with. Maybe something is grinding in the relationship that we can't quite put our finger on. Or maybe something is binding us together, like decisions to blend or compromise, but we're not fully conscious of these changes. Sometimes it is the tensions that feel pronounced, while the signs of intimacy and connectedness can be taken for granted. Because it can seem so natural, we don't account for the growth that was happening through our small glances or touches or observations.

And although we are both in the same relationship, these changes are never experienced in the same way. We are like instruments, one made of oak and another of birch. As the humidity and temperature shift, we adapt and bend in unique ways. The wood of our lives is our respective stories, the joys we've seen, the insecurities we've harbored, or the obstacles we've had to overcome. With each passing season, we carry what we were and what we had become, whether successful or dysfunctional, into the next season.

When things begin to shift and we start to feel the stretching—which sometimes feels like tearing—it is never an easy process. Sometimes it might feel like it's the person you're with who doesn't seem to fit or who seems to irritate. Sometimes it might feel like the job isn't right or we're in the wrong town or our family is either too close or too far away.

And often it isn't just our own inner world or familial circles that press us. The way the world renders some bodies invisible in one moment and hypervisible in another, ways that we see privilege boost up some people while we scrape and claw for every inch—systems of oppression and silencing are always pressing in. As we have gotten older, we have discovered the power and insidiousness of these systems.

We are navigating all of it, the individual, the interpersonal, and the social. It's in those moments of stretching that the sinews of ourselves stretch in ways we do not expect. Part of building a life together is acknowledging that we do not know the ways we are growing or the forces that are pulling or pushing us. But when we recognize that change is inevitable, we can begin to look for the signs or opportunities to stretch—or to at least warm up before something gets torn.

While there's a healthy market full of self-help books and personality tests to help us "get to know ourselves," part of the challenge in a relationship is learning who you are *with the other person.* It's like the difference between trying to do a squat on solid ground and trying to do a squat on a balance board. On solid ground the motion seems straightforward. But on the balance board you have to engage your stomach muscles and your back, and there is the definite possibility of falling. But being committed in a relationship is also being committed and open to self-reflection about who you are, and who you are with this person, and opening up to the possibilities and acknowledging the strains those discoveries will reveal.

We've seen a lot of people, especially a lot of young couples, hope for a plan. Especially for couples who are married after living on their own for a good part of their life, we hear again and again about having to manage and negotiate expectations.

We are inundated with tools for evaluating ourselves and how-to manuals for just about anything we can imagine.

To be sure, there is a place for plans and preparation. But part of adequately planning is also recognizing the limitations of any given circumstance. When we begin to think about the persons who enter into a relationship, we begin to see just how little we know about ourselves. Ironically, learning one's self is also about embracing what can't be known—the uncertainty of changes before us, of what we might discover as we explore how our past or our social space or our bodies shape the way we experience the world. Learning one's self is embracing the mystery and depth we each hold within us—a process that continues throughout our lives.

No Model to Follow

There aren't many advantages to having no money, no long-standing family traditions, and no fundamental stability in the home. In a way, these all were connected to one another and to the difficult relationships our parents had while we were growing up.

My (Gail's) parents struggled to assimilate. My father spent most of his time and energy at home (outside of his job and ministry), staying safe within the local Korean community. My mom, on the other hand, almost feverishly tried to embrace what "American life" (read: proximate to middle-class white people) meant to her. She had an incredible imagination for greater opportunities and a degree of freedom to pursue her call. But my parents were eleven years apart in age as well, which my mom often suggested felt like a generational difference.

Their marriage had unstable and challenging moments for much of my childhood. So when my mom packed up her things and left for seminary in another state when I was eleven, the news wasn't surprising. Was it hard and sad? Did I cry myself to sleep often? Did I think I was dying when I got my period at school that semester she was gone? Of course. I was eleven. Life in my home rarely felt predictable, much less filled with traditions I looked forward to. This left little room for instilling in me what a thriving married life looked like, or at least an image of something I would want for myself.

Traditions were faint and inconsistent in my (Brian's) childhood. My mom and dad were divorced by the time I was eight. My dad was in and out of our lives depending on his state of sobriety and financial security. But somehow they were always friends. Maybe that's what made it all so strange. Within any given year we might go from my dad visiting on Thursday nights so that he could watch *Knots Landing* and *Dallas* with my mom to then not seeing him for months and only knowing the state of things because of my mom's increased stress over money.

For both of us, the only tradition was the uncertainty that seemed to fill our childhood. New houses, new living situations, schools, maybe a vacation, but more than likely time away was visiting a relative for a week or two. This is not to say that our parents didn't instill some beautiful things in our lives. But those lessons or strengths or inclinations weren't really a result of how they lived together for our sake. In a way, our parents were trying their best, seeming to fight their own demons while also trying to show us love in the best way they could.

We have always been looking for those models, to see some semblance of what life together might look like. More than likely the ideal was never really there in the first place. So we had to make our own image, cobble together the little pieces of what we glimpsed or what we wanted to avoid, and patch it together until it fit us.

The Certainty of Change

As we finish chapter 1, we invite you to self-reflection and, more important, to reimagining who you are even as you discover the person you're with. This process begins by flipping one's perspective about certainty, resisting the lure of the static, and embracing ourselves and each other as dynamic creatures.

Because we were married so young with no models of "success," we didn't have much of a plan. For us, the plan was simply to get to the next thing and figure it out from there. The clearest part of the plan was to not recreate the pain of our childhood homes, while holding on to the small joys or patterns of love that were present.

Part of what gave us the freedom to live with that posture was recognizing the changes that had already happened in each of us, even in the few years of knowing one another. We might have had some semblance of a plan when we were nineteen, but in our first few conversations, we could see we were changing and that there was so much life in what was growing within us and between us. The possibility of ongoing change felt more hopeful than scary. Whether jumping from a lifetime of training to follow a call, or accepting an invitation to a fish fry, or deciding to have children, we had not only seen the scary uncertainty but also the harvest of what that change made possible in our lives and in our relationships.

Most of all, by accepting the flip from the certainty of a plan or a prescribed goal to the certainty of change, we could recognize that the other person was going to change. We knew we were not going to be the same people we talked to on the phone in those early days. And we couldn't control who the other person was going to be. There was no plan for personal growth any more than there was a plan for familial life or vocation. There was only a direction, toward and with one another.

The power of the flip allows us to see the possibilities in the shifts and tensions that emerge. Rather than the tensions being a deviation from or an obstacle to the plan, they become moments to sound one another out, to take stock, and to see how our lives together might open to new possibilities.

Discussion Questions

- What have you discovered about yourself because of the person you're with?
- Has anything you've discovered scared you?
- What's been enriching?
- What have the unplanned parts of your life taught you about yourself?

The static holds on to whatever makes us feel safe or seen or comfortable or unchallenged. Sometimes we need these responses simply to get through difficult times. But what happens when we grow accustomed to the terror or the discomfort and live feeling afraid to let that go for something more?

A static personhood tries to maintain the tethers of its personhood because it only knows itself in relationship to those connections. But sometimes those tethers also preclude or block the possibilities of new connections and new experiences that allow us to discover new aspects of who we are or who we might become.

Discussion Questions

- In what areas of your life do you feel like it's safer to stay the same rather than risk something new?

A dynamic view of personhood (and relationships) sees the possibility of relationships, experiences, stretches, and shifts as an opportunity to live in the fullness of the world and contribute to it. But it never happens without some pain. And while this idea might seem like it is simply resisting the lure of the static, it's slightly different because it asks us to make a fundamentally different assumption about who we are and who we are going to be. When we feel ourselves beginning to change, we might experience this initially as loss, especially in a relationship. But what if we assume that change is a part of who we are?

Discussion Questions

- In what areas of your life have you sensed change?
- What have these changes added to your life?
- What have these changes added to your relationship?

TWO

Learning
the Other

S elf-reflection might seem like an odd place to open a chapter on learning another person. But self-reflection is tied to learning the person you share life with because we can never take for granted that we know ourselves fully, either who we were, who we are, or who we will be.

I (Brian) always thought of myself as a sensitive guy. I was raised by a single mother and lived large chunks of my childhood in a house full of women. I heard all their stories of comments they'd received and of the ways my mom and aunts had been treated at work. My mom encouraged us to go to therapy when we were teenagers. I was always talking about my feelings and reflecting on why I had done or not done something. And yet, so often my self-reflection tilts toward self-rationalization. Insecurity or uncertainty can awaken curiosity and humility, but it can also harden the walls that protect the ideas we have about ourselves. Self-reflection is a risky act that asks us to wrestle with the possibility that we did not handle a situation perfectly and that we could stand to grow in the way we respond to situations and people.

Self-reflection is akin to the Christian idea of confession. We don't mean confession in the sense of creating a laundry list of the ways we have failed. Rather, we mean it in the sense of Augustine's work by the same name. There, confession has two meanings. The first is confessing who God is, the one Augustine's heart restlessly seeks. Confession is to say, "God, you are . . ." The second meaning is confessing who we are: "God, I am . . ." These two statements are related to one another, calling and responding, shaping how we imagine God and how we imagine ourselves.

Confession in this way doesn't have to be, "You, God, are so amazing, and I am dirt." But even in this distorted sense of confession, we see the relational aspect of identifying our shortcomings, because there is always a relationship that we have violated. The negative claim we are making also reflects a hope, something that we aspire to be in relation to God and others.

When we connect this to confession in the Christian life as the combination of the "We believe" of the creeds and of "God forgive me, for I have sinned," we see the reciprocal nature of confession as both self-reflection and relationality. We consider who we are, and we consider the one we are with.

Confession also allows us to enter difficult conversations as moments of discovery rather than a battle to be won. One of the biggest challenges in relational conflict is to acknowledge the complexity of the other person and ourselves. We are frustrated or tired or hurt, and it is easy to ask why the other person cannot see what we see, or why they are not doing what we would like to be done. When we see disagreements as a tug-of-war where we cannot give ground, we also lose the opportunity to discover something of the person we share life with.

In a relationship where two people share the mundane and the life-changing, learning the other person is always going to be a process of recalibrating the tools we use to see and understand who this person is. But in this case, *we* are the tool, and like trying to observe the stars in the sky, we always have to adjust for the fact that we sit on a spinning marble of rock and are constantly moving. The seasons shift, the weather changes, and through it all, we are trying to discern the same stars. If we are to learn the other person, we must also account for the ways we are changing. We must confess the ways we ourselves are moving.

Gail

Our life together has been a continual learning process.

During our first five-hour phone call, connecting with Brian felt easy. When we finally met in person two months later, after dozens of letters and even more hours on the phone, it seemed odd to speak to each other in the flesh. At that time, things like video apps and social media weren't available to help me figure out his vibe before meeting in person.

After taking a thirteen-hour bus ride from Rochester to Harrisburg, Pennsylvania, I was picked up by Brian and our mutual friend, and we headed off to visit Brian's family for Thanksgiving. Throughout that awkward first meeting and car ride, it seemed more natural for both of us to look straight ahead while catching up. As soon as one of us looked over and saw that the voice wasn't coming through the phone, we'd sense the strangeness and stop talking.

Later, when I moved in with Brian's family during the summer of 1995, I discovered who he was around his family. And the learning didn't stop there but continued as we navigated our first post-marriage living situation, as we had to make our first big decision about career choices, and as we found out we were having our first child. The learning continued as we made a decision about grad school, as I saw who Brian was *in* grad school, and then as I learned who he was in a steady job and career after more than a decade of juggling multiple jobs while living the in-between life of a grad student.

It's one thing to figure out your own likes and dislikes, to grasp who you are and who you want to be. But the dynamics change when you're in a relationship. The arc of an intention or a frustration begins to slide in unexpected ways when you're with the other person day in and day out. As we begin to learn who we are, we are also learning who we are *with* this other person. On this journey together, we are rediscovering our own stories and histories and tendencies, and we are also learning about this person with us, in their unfolding and discovery.

Learning about one another is one of the most foundational parts of a relationship. It doesn't make much sense to even talk about this as a "step." "Of course we have to learn about one another!" you might think. But there's a difference between learning about a static and unchanging topic and learning about *someone* who is dynamic and shifting. The person we are with is not a table that can be disassembled to see how it's put together. He or she is not a tree with a prescribed amount of light and nutrients that are optimal for growth and that simply need to be memorized and applied.

Instead, people are both static and dynamic. There are aspects of who we are that will remain, while parts of who we are will change or adapt to the pressures of life. For example, I have always been uber-social, but having three kids and leading in ministry for more than two decades have allowed me to appreciate and even crave time to myself. What I need has changed over time, especially as I grew deeper into the work of full-time ministry. And as I have changed in my social needs and wants, Brian has also had to learn the person I have become as a pastor.

The people we journey with, especially in committed, intimate relationships, are not who they are always going to be. As much as personality tests like Myers-Briggs and the Enneagram reveal underlying qualities, bents, or preferences, how we inhabit those preferences and tendencies will shift over time.

To learn one another is to recognize that we all change, including the person we are with. Learning one another is an ongoing process of reflection, conversation, taking stock, being patient, stretching, and asking the one we are with to stretch with us. This process can sometimes be painful; sometimes it feels like the other person is stretching away from us. There may be less to talk about or fewer shared hobbies. Or maybe you'll find that the way you each approach uncertainty has shifted because one person got burned or hurt and now is nervous or cautious, while the other is still willing to take chances.

Learning the other can feel unnerving because it means having to admit there are things you don't know. And even when you think you know them, sometimes they surprise you with how they've changed.

When we were barely older than teenagers, the idea of change and learning one another wasn't a shock. We hadn't lived on our own, and we were still figuring out our sense of call and vocation. Living on shoestring budgets meant very little freedom to discover new things beyond a different kind of snack at the grocery store or the new clothing store at the mall. Early on, our world was very small. But because we met so young, there were also lots of changes to come and a lot to learn, and twenty-five years later, there's a lot that we are still learning about this person we've chosen to share our lives with.

Early on, we each knew we needed to be attentive to who this other person was, learning their story and how they were wired, but also figuring out how the other's who-ness mingled with the other's own. Neither of us had many reference points because we had never really known life without the other.

Seeing the other person can be hard, especially as we get older. Our stories and patterns become deeply grooved in how we walk in the world. Becoming a student of the one we are

33

with means seeing who they are and who they might become and all the changes along the way.

Who Are You?

Before we think about the other person, it's important to note how our own history and identity shape how we perceive him or her. It's all fine and good to talk about "learning" the other person, but if we don't have the language to describe what we're seeing, or if a part of our own history shapes how we interpret someone else's behavior, we will tend to pass over a detail or a story or a pattern and assume we know the cause. We have to sit with ourselves and our stories before we can begin the work of learning the other.

In premarital meetings with couples, I (Gail) often use an exercise called "Who Are You?" The exercise not only helps people tease out why they do the things they do, but in their recalling and telling, it also allows the other person to hear the *why* behind what that person does and the deeper history they carry. It goes something like this:

- Recall a memory that typifies your *relationships* growing up. How did you engage with parents, siblings, extended family, neighbors, and so on? Were the relationships gregarious? Subdued? Tense? Abusive? Fun-loving? Strict?
  a. **Ways of doing**: How or in what ways do you replicate this behavior today? Or how have you been formed?
- Recall a memory that typifies how your family *thought* about things. Were family conversations usually hopeful, pessimistic, positive, judgmental, racist, closed-minded, or generous?
  b. **Ways of thinking**: How or in what ways do you replicate this behavior? Or how have you been formed?

34

People don't just happen. Most of us don't make up how we will respond to the world and each other out of nowhere. We learn how to respond to the world and relate to each other from our environment. We are how we are and who we have become because of many influences and experiences over a lifetime—both in positive ways and through acts of resistance and negation.

Gail

When I think about the decades of peeling back the layers in Brian's story, it not only helps me appreciate who he is now but also allows me greater capacity for more grace, patience, understanding, and advocacy. I remember one particular premarital counseling session when the pastor discussed the results of our Myers-Briggs personality tests to help us better understand each other. This was a few weeks before our wedding.

"Brian, it looks like you're a fairly firm introvert, and Gail . . . well, you're quite the opposite," he noted. Those simple words opened a new chapter in our relationship of assumptions and expectations—you know, the ones where couples tend to project affinities and objections based on personality tests. "Why do you always drag your feet when it's time to go to my staff Christmas party?" I'd ask. Or, "Why do you always fall asleep right before we're about to host our small group at the house? If you don't want to host these gatherings, just say so!" This behavior seemed so ridiculously passive-aggressive. "Just say so!" was what I'd always say, whether out loud or in my head, as I gave him a side-eye and kept it pushing. These moments would be infuriating at times, and quite frankly, from my perspective, it seemed as if it *only* happened when it was for my engagements or for the gatherings I initiated. Isn't that always the way?

As the years passed and these moments layered upon each other, I began to notice patterns. From the moment he and

I started dating, Brian told me about suffering constant ear infections that necessitated surgery when he was eight years old, which left him with significant hearing loss in his left ear. Over time, I would notice moments when we were at a gathering or a restaurant where he seemed to be straining to hear the conversation over the background music or would be frustrated by the hum all around us. When we sat in theaters or went for walks, he always moved to my left side so he could hear me better. When the boys were young and they would whisper in their dad's left ear and stare at him, waiting for a response, I'd often say to them, "Baby, you have to say it louder because Dad can't hear you in that ear."

The summer when I lived with Brian and his family, I had asked Brian if we could go to the Washington Mall for the annual Fourth of July festivities. I had always loved crowded celebratory gatherings like state fairs, amusement parks, and festivals. Little did I know that such gatherings were a *nightmare* for him. Of course, he kindly said, "Yes, I'll take you." But a couple hours before we left the house, he was nowhere to be found. It didn't take long to discover where he was: stuck in the bathroom with anxiety-riddled stomach issues. Mind you, this wasn't the first time our plans had been foiled by a similar situation. The ignorant and ungenerous part of me blurted out, "Why do you always do this?! If you don't want to go, just say so!" Or worse, "Why can't you time this and take care of it earlier?"

Fast-forward, and I've learned that for most of Brian's childhood, living in a loving but constantly shifting environment and reality—eight homes in seventeen years, teased throughout elementary and middle school, parents' divorce, his dad's alcoholism, and his dad's death—took a toll on Brian's body. Stomach issues were his body's way of dealing with stress and anxiety. In learning this about Brian and by growing aware of how his hearing loss could also cause incredible anxiety in public, I've come to see that his social angst isn't necessarily about introversion. Sometimes our story, our experiences, our realities, when pressed over time, cause us to navigate the world in ways we can't quite articulate or express to a loved one. Not only does learning the other mean gaining particular knowledge about that person; it also calls out action and advocacy on our part. Empathy leads to different decisions.

Over the years, I've learned to decline certain joint invitations if it means that Brian will struggle to participate. I've learned to save the seat on my left—always—whenever there's an occasion for saving seats in crowded spaces. I've learned to set him up at a restaurant so that his good ear will face the most people at our table. The beauty in learning the other is that it transforms us. And our transformation is not just for our own sake; it also enables the greater good of the whole.

Having a son who is also physically affected by stress, I have grown aware that one's responses to something in the moment don't always correspond to one's desire for it. Our whole body and being is a product of our story. But we are also more than any single response we can offer in the moment.

This was especially important for me to grasp because, even as I was learning and discovering things about Brian, I was also learning things about myself. I had to confront the fact that I didn't grow up with parents who extended much grace to me. It was a life of hustle, during which we weren't allowed to stay home from school just because we had a 101-degree fever. Mine was a "do it sick anyway" upbringing. In fact, I remember being allowed to stay home from school only when I broke my leg. We didn't have insurance, so I lay on the couch until I could wrap up my leg and put a little pressure on it to make it through a whole day at school. It was brutal. But it was my reality. And in many ways, it led me to harbor an unhealthy expectation of that grit and hustle and to project that expectation onto everyone around me.

Brian has taught me a lot about grace and what it means to be human in all of its beauty, frailties, and imperfections. As much as I thought I needed to be ten times better, stronger, and more resilient than everyone around me (to be seen, to be heard), that kind of facade isn't sustainable. And, by God's grace, I found myself with a partner who never played that game or allowed me to get sucked into it. Brian has taught me that we can be gracious with others only when we are gracious with ourselves.

Discussion Questions

- What are little things about the other person that get under your skin that you haven't asked about?
- That maybe you've made some assumptions about?
- How has your own upbringing shaped those assumptions?

Brian

Every couple is different. And we knew about some of our differences in our first years of dating. But the first twenty-four hours of our married life could not have made these differences more apparent.

We arrived at the door of our new apartment and pulled our few boxes and futon into the 400-square-foot studio. I was ready to lounge and grab some food. Gail was ready to unpack, decorate, and make this home. Little did I know that what she meant was that everything was going to be out of boxes, pictures would be hung, pots and towels and curtains would all be purchased and set up . . . before we slept. "We don't sleep until this is home." And this would be her pattern in every move since.

The next morning after that first move, I heard some soft coughing, a few heavy sighs. I opened my eyes, and there was

Gail, eyes wide open, staring at me. "Are you up? It's sooooooooo late!" she said.

"It's 7:30 in the morning, love."

"We need to get up or we're going to waste the day. What should we do?"

"Everything is still closed . . ."

"But still. I'm lonely."

Completion. Anticipation. A plan. Together. These were the first things I learned about Gail as we started to build our life together. She wanted to completely finish one thing before moving on to another. She wanted to enjoy everything she could every day. She wanted to have a plan that she could anticipate and get excited for. And whatever she did, she wanted us to do it together.

I was a bit more "play it by ear"—the kind of person who'd say, "Let's wake up around 11 or 12, eat some brunch, and see what the day brings." You can see the challenge, right?

Every couple has to navigate personality differences like these. Learning Gail meant beginning to attend to the ways she ordered her world and finding ways I could contribute to that order, not just dismantle it.

I came to realize that Gail's planning was never about control or a need to know. She tended to plan because she saw a lot. I mean *a lot*. She was able to see what was happening that week, in the next few months, and far beyond. In the midst of everything she saw, she also saw the opportunities to rest, or to go on vacation, or just to decompress. And she cannot rest if she knows a job isn't finished or there are boxes left to unpack.

As much as I love a spontaneous trip or walk, I know that if Gail hasn't finished the task at hand, the trip or the treat will not be relaxing or fun. In the small things, every day, our life together gave me a chance to learn how she operated so that I could partner with her and help her feel seen and supported. For me, there's nothing better than a distraction while we're unpacking ("Let's go get McDonald's!"); for her, there is joy when the job is done. And in the midst of it all, she wants to be together. Drink coffee. Get a snack. Go to the grocery store . . . together.

Over time, we have both softened our edges. I get up earlier (without her needing to wake me!); she can relax in the midst of a project or leave some boxes unpacked. She can endure a few hours away from me while I'm on a bike ride, even though I know it's still itching her insides a bit. And I know that when she is stressed or feeling like there are too many things to hold, she is going to need help finishing the job before she can rest or take some time off. Learning one another's quirks and tendencies, seeing them as part of how our partner is wired, allows us to value the way their gifts and strengths add to the home, even as those differences can stretch us.

Sometimes the most intense moments of learning come amid conflict. Some of Gail's and my earliest arguments took on a familiar pattern. Gail, usually talkative and eager to share a thought or an idea, would grow quiet. I would find her cleaning something or going on a walk or running errands by herself. Picking up the signal that she was upset, I would badger her to talk about it until she finally did. Then I would turn around and accuse her of some slight, bringing up the ten things I had been sitting on for the last three months that were completely unrelated to what she was upset about. We would be quiet and barely talk for a day (sometimes two if it was bad), and then we'd apologize and talk through what had led up to the argument.

What kept me from hearing Gail was my tendency to feel any criticism as an attack. I had been teased as a kid and tried to be as quiet as possible in classes, trying to follow every rule. As my mom struggled with depression, I operated like a barometer in the house, feeling out any subtle change and trying to clean or help out when I saw she was welling up or getting frustrated. I was the good kid, the one who helped, who saw, who wasn't like the "other" kids. Any type of criticism shattered who I thought I was.

All this meant that I was also very prickly when it came to criticism that I felt was unfounded. So whenever Gail would get upset or frustrated, I would feel like she didn't see all the things I was thinking or doing for her. I was lost in my own interpretation of our lives. And because I was so lost in my insecurities, I never really heard or learned what her worries or frustrations were, or how she was experiencing our relationship in that moment.

As we got older and I began to have a better sense of who I was, I also started to see what was underneath some of Gail's worries or concerns or frustrations. This is not to say that I don't still struggle with insecurities, but I recognize there are some aspects of my story that keep me from seeing and being present to Gail in difficult moments. Learning yourself in order to learn the other person means beginning to ask why certain patterns persist.

Discussion Questions

- What are the moments you got upset when your partner raised an issue or a frustration?
- What kept you from hearing their concern or hurt?

Ways to Learn the Other

There are many ways to become attentive to the one you're with. Using therapy, professional counselors are trained to help you recognize patterns in your life, while couples counselors are trained to wrestle with how each person is seeing and hearing and sensing the other. Personality tests help do much of the same. While not always scientific, personality tests can be great conversation starters. Talking about past events and why a certain conversation keeps arising is a wonderful though often difficult way of seeing how each person experienced a specific moment and what they felt. But how someone navigates their own introversion or extroversion, how they cope with pain and disappointment, or how willing they are to try new things can change over time.

Anyone who has spent a long time with a child knows that change is inevitable. Infants seem to transform even week to week. Just when a sleep schedule's in place and you've gotten the swing of the rocker just right, you figure out they like to be patted on the back instead of rubbed in a circular pattern. Then, seemingly overnight, they don't want to be touched, or they need the rabbit instead of the bear. Raising children is more like tending a garden than building a bookshelf.

Yet in the midst of those changes, we can see certain threads of personality. And we are still those children. As we mature, we have plenty of tools that help us identify our personality types, our work habits, and so on. But we don't have many tools to understand how these aspects of who we are affect living and binding ourselves to someone else—and how the other person inevitably changes us. This cycle continues: as we evolve, the person we are with evolves, and as they change, we adapt and push and pull. This cycle of growth and adaptation is a reality of what it means to live together.

We opened this chapter with stories from our early years, of times when we felt a bit like children, like each year brought new changes and discoveries of ourselves and the other person. But even as we have entered our mid-forties, we continue to discover new facets of the other, and of ourselves. Sometimes these discoveries and changes were beautiful, and our years together allowed us to settle in with one another in a new phase of life or in the midst of upheaval, or even in moments of rest. But other times have found us in the midst of some of the hardest conversations and arguments of our whole marriage. We can tend to get used to the person who has been with us for so long, and then a job change or an emptier house make clear what had been somewhat hidden. Maybe the other person has changed, or maybe I've changed.

Continually choosing each other means relearning the one we've committed to. And this is an ongoing cycle of reflection, observation, and conversation that requires trust and honesty and the courage to ask difficult questions. As you continue to learn about yourself and the person you're with, consider digging deeper in these two areas: (1) observing each other's patterns and (2) learning how the other person has navigated systemic realities, including race, gender, sexuality, ability, and class.

Observing Patterns

Working as an executive pastor for many years, I (Gail) saw it as my primary job to learn how to read the lead pastor so that I could most accurately represent them and their vision for the church and respond to inquiries on their behalf. To read them well was an act of care—to figure out when they would best receive new input or ideas or when it was most helpful to share difficult news. It was important for me to learn their patterns and inclinations during both static and pressed situations, especially when confronted by change. What kinds of scenarios might cause undue stress? When were there opportunities for encouragement? I was constantly reading and learning, not only so that I could do my job well but also for the good and health of the organization.

Learning to notice the patterns of the other, whatever the nature of the relationship, will inevitably help us to look out for the good of the whole—the wider family, the friend circle, the marriage, the staff, the team, and so on. Unfortunately, in dominant white American culture that celebrates rugged individualism, we can too readily undermine the power of learning the other as a communal act. Koreans embrace and value this notion of a sixth sense, called 눈치, or nunchi. Loosely translated, nunchi is the subtle ability to gauge another's mood and feelings, otherwise known as emotional intelligence. Korean culture cultivates, starting at an early age, a heightened sense of situational awareness, or nunchi, a capacity for anticipating another person's needs preemptively, before the need is voiced. In many ways, nunchi exemplifies a culture that deeply values community and the well-being of the whole.

After about ten years of marriage, Gail and I (Brian) had seen our fair share of challenges—not enough money, Gail feeling stretched with kids, worries about our jobs and callings. We began to see a pattern when figuring out how to move forward. Gail's first instinct was always to conquer, make a change, shift the board. For her, circumstances were not going to dictate what our options were. For me, the tendency was to bend and wait, trying to make the best out of what was available and taking advantage of any opportunities that came my way.

Clearly, these were not terribly compatible strategies, but after a while, we started to see a similar conversation emerge, and it trickled into the smaller tasks that any challenge required. Whenever it came time to move to a new apartment or house, Gail was constantly searching ads, noting rents, figuring out timing. Meanwhile, I was sitting back and waiting until it got closer to the move date, feeling a little overwhelmed by all the options and generally settling for what was familiar. But for Gail, the opportunity to move was also the opportunity to improve some aspect of our living situation (usually for the same rent!).

In actuality, both her patterns and mine have positive and negative attributes. Gail's approach meant we had every possible apartment listed and planned for. But part of Gail's approach was also about trying to maintain control in uncertain moments. While my approach allowed for some flexibility, it was also rooted in not working through a certain paralysis I experienced with the prospect of change. So here Gail was, working furiously to find us a new home, and there I was, paralyzed and blankly staring into the distance.

When it came to packing, though, Gail was usually overwhelmed, and suddenly I would spring into action. Eventually, we came to see these tendencies not as inadequacies but as particular ways we each occupy our world. At the same time, recognizing our patterns also helped us see the areas where we needed to put in more effort or needed to contribute more so that the other person didn't bear the entire burden at any given time.

Tensions don't always get figured out so easily, though. We don't always make it to the aha moments, even twenty-five years in. For example, why do we get into our most heated arguments on vacations? We like to call them "intense fellowship" because that sounds softer, but in truth, we argue, and I (Gail) end up spending at least half a day ignoring Brian in what I call "silent fellowship." To this day, we cannot seem to reconcile the fact that I like to see and explore new things and go to new places when I am away from work. And to make things even more complicated, because my everyday job requires me to plan ahead and coordinate and research options and care for lots of people, usually six to twelve months out at a time, I need someone else to coordinate the vacation. (Do you feel me?) Otherwise, it just feels like work in a different setting, with different people.

Brian likes to chill. Like, *chill*. Like, take the first few days to scope everything out and figure out what we could or should do—then chill some more. "I only have seven days, babe!" I'd gently scream through my teeth. "I'm gonna need you to chill on the way there so we can pound the pavement when we arrive!" Vacations to me are maximizing and discovering what is available to us at that particular place, whether it's visiting the local hole-in-the-wall restaurants or shops, kayaking, strolling downtown at night, checking out the scene, or hitting the various beaches if that's where we're at—you know, vacationing! And that is Brian's nightmare. New things and busy social scenes are a literal nightmare for him. I know this. And yet.

For me (Brian), vacations are a chance to get away, to rest and enjoy your people, a time when you shouldn't have to make any decisions or figure out anything new. Just soak in a pool, rest on the beach, read a book, ride a bike. Gail and I have yet to have a vacation like this. After twenty-five years, you would think we would know what the other person wanted and was hoping for. But somehow the first few days always begin with that dreaded question: "So, what are we going to do today?" When Gail asks, I know I'm already too far gone because I haven't figured out somewhere new to go or what the local excitement is. When I scramble for a few ideas that might come to me in that moment, everything goes silent—for a day, or even two. After that, it's a delicate dance. I know it by heart. (I have the conversation practically memorized!) We each enact our respective steps, until it's time to plan the next vacation.

This tension has only gotten more pronounced. We're more financially stable and able to choose our vacations with more freedom. It was easier when the only option was the off-season special at Myrtle Beach. We also know ourselves a bit more now. Gail works hard, grinds day in and day out, and wants to make good use of her few weeks of vacation. She is a play-hard, rest-hard person. But she also spends much of her work time planning, organizing, and being the social woo of her job. Ideally, her vacation would be a place that is new and exciting and planned completely by someone else.

As I've gotten older, I've come to love the woods and nature, bike rides, and hikes. Maybe a bookstore or an art museum. But definitely nothing new. New freaks me out.

You can probably sense the difficulty.

We wrote these accounts of our vacation separately, but it should be pretty clear that we know one another. And in knowing what the other person is going through and needs, you would think we would be able to avoid yearly summer blowouts on vacation, right? As much as we would both love for that to be true, we know that life together is not just solving problems in order to resolve all tension. It is also realizing that some aspects of each person are really incompatible with the other person, and that our needs will shift over time as things change with jobs, kids, and community life. Yet we still have to find a way.

An easy formula for resolving these kinds of conflicts would be ideal, but we don't have one. That said, we are honest about what we need, about what we are willing to do, and what we would really rather not do. We have also been together long enough to know that these tensions may not persist. Gail might come to love bike rides. Brian might come to love new adventures. But until then, we also trust one another to be willing to stretch for the other and find some spaces of respite and joy on the journey.

Discussion Questions

- What are the other person's patterns? When pressed? When confronted by the prospect of change? In times of "plenty"?

Navigating Systemic Realities

All of us live inside vast, complicated social histories. Race, ethnicity, gender, ability, sexuality, and class are all systemic realities that are lived day-to-day and moment-to-moment. We live in families and communities that have shaped how we see who we are and how we ought to recognize and either resist or accommodate these realities. We'll dive further into the significance of racial and gender formation in the next few chapters. For now, our focus will be on the ways that learning the other means entering into that person's deeper social formation.

Gail

I was initially drawn to Brian in part because of our seemingly shared experiences of cultural and racial in-betweenness, always questioning our sense of belonging wherever we were. As a child of Korean immigrant parents, I've navigated the complexities of language and of cultural differences in a variety of spaces, from home to school to neighborhood. I found belonging within the Black church as a teenager. Brian would share his stories with me about being a biracial (Black/white) child primarily raised by his white mother and her side of the family, even while learning and becoming aware of the work his brown body was doing in the world as he grew older. We shared this in-betweenness from the beginning.

Whenever we find ourselves in public spaces, whether at church or at the Korean grocery store or while walking down the street, I find myself noticing other people's stares, glares, fears, suspicions, or curiosity about Brian. I've also noticed when we've been in predominantly Black spaces over the years—like our children's elementary school in North Carolina, or Black churches, or gatherings within the community—that I see Brian's angst, his questions about whether he'll be welcomed or seen as "Black enough."

These experiences have opened my eyes to the ways we *all* have stories and experiences that slowly inform who we are and how we see ourselves and negotiate our way through the world. While I've named how learning the particularities of Brian's identity as a Black man is part of my growth in our relationship, there are many aspects of one's story and the often-complicated intersections of gender, culture, sexuality, and ability as well that require attentiveness and care for any relationship to truly flourish.

When our kids were younger and loved playing with LEGO sets, I remember seeing the picture of the Star Wars Millennium Falcon on the cover of the box and having a rough idea of how this thing was going to get built. But if you've ever had the joy of building LEGO sets with your child, you've quickly realized that the beginning stages of the building process are nothing like what you imagined. Why? Because there are pieces you didn't even know existed. Why? Because it's a part of the inside of the spaceship that you'll never see in its finished form. Why? Because it's either part of the fancy detailing of the ship, or it helps create stability for that part of the wing . . . from the inside! If we approach every person and relationship with this kind of "clean slate" mentality, or with an understanding that the internal realities of one's being hold surprising complexity, we'll more readily avoid the temptation to assume "all men" or "all ____ people" should naturally be a particular way or possess certain instincts (e.g., women are nurturing, Asian women are submissive, Black men are dangerous, men can fix cars, women can cook). Start with step one and learn to discover the other person from their beginnings, and how every piece informs their larger story.

Brian

While I grew up in a house of women, I still had so much to learn from life alongside Gail. When we started dating, I happened to be doing a project in a Christian education class that required church visits, and I was visiting a Korean church.

In many ways it was a typical Korean immigrant church with a service in Korean and a service in English, a youth group, and a lunch after the service that had a good number of women cooking during the service. This was part of Gail's upbringing.

But I had to learn the history of pale skin to understand why so many Koreans thought she wasn't 100 percent Korean with her slightly darker complexion to see that her experience of the Korean church and the Korean community was a complicated one that had a lot to do with her being a strong woman. And these forms of alienation were a big reason for her finding a sense of place and home in the Black community and the Black church.

She is Korean because . . . she *is* Korean (surprise!). But she also embodies particular markers of Korean culture in small, sometimes imperceptible ways. For example, Gail has a sense of communal responsibility, she values celebration around food (and in abundance), and she has a deep devotion to family. But her life was also about resisting conformity to the ideals Korean culture sometimes asked her to inhabit. Learning Gail also meant learning about the tensions of accommodation and assimilation in immigrant communities, the legacies of patriarchy, and how Black life had been a home for people looking for safe harbor.

I did not sit down with books, reading and studying for hours to learn these lessons. But I did have to learn not to assume that her hesitation about a certain restaurant or refusal to speak Korean to another Korean was just an individual decision. Sometimes we talked about those moments, and other times we were both discovering along the way as we reflected about any given "why" on our journey together.

Discussion Questions

- Think about some of your responses or conversation about the earlier discussion questions. How many of those were shaped by realities of race, ethnicity, gender, ability, or sexuality?
- What are the stories and histories you need to learn in order to understand where the tendencies of your partner might come from?

Learning the other person requires a posture of humility and wonder. In writing this, we realize we may have emphasized how tension or disagreement can sometimes be the way we come to discover who this other person is. But equally beautiful are the moments when we learn how delighted the other person is when we bring home their favorite soda or plan a trip on the weekend. Learning the other means a loving attentiveness that opens us to new wonders and joys, seen through the eyes of the other. It means discovering how they are growing and changing through the years. Life together will always mean a lifelong journey of learning.

THREE

Race and Belonging

Part of what connected us was not only our love of laughter and conversation but also our experience navigating in-between spaces of race. At first glance, the connection between a Black, mixed-race boy from Maryland and a Korean American girl from Illinois and Oklahoma doesn't seem to have much ethnic or racial overlap. But we were both navigating the larger forces and legacies of race in our homes and communities.

Race is not simply a set of biological markers, nor is ethnicity reducible to language or customs or country of origin. Race and ethnicity are laced with complicated threads of belonging and power, exclusion and expectation. As children we don't always see these threads or feel the forces so bluntly. But as we get older, we discover how our bodies are being "read" and all the accompanying expectations or fears.

Learning ourselves and one another means examining how race has shaped us and is continuing to shape us. In some ways, it would have been wonderful if our lives together could be a hermetically sealed chamber where it was "just us." But that is never the case. As an example, it didn't take long for me (Brian) to realize that Gail's connection and sense of belonging in the Black church and community was linked to her struggle with belonging in the Korean community, a community that was working out its own sense of citizenship and loss that stretched between histories of colonization and occupation in Korea and seeking to build new lives in a United States that saw them as foreigners.

This navigation was always present with us, whether in the presence of food, in witnessing questioning looks in Korean restaurants and grocery stores, or in overhearing others' hushed conversations. It was even more present when we began expressing our inner hopes and frustrations, something Gail's home rarely made space for. And it was especially present when we had children and had to wrestle with whether to teach the boys Korean or send them to Korean school.

How does race shape us? Race, in itself, is not real. It is a historical construct invented by European theologians, scientists, philosophers, and colonizers to make sense of themselves. This was not always an explicit exercise but arose from encounters with people and places that were different from them. In their attempt to account for these differences, they used themselves as norms, as ideals, and described others in relationships of inferiority to the ideal of the European man.

Ways of understanding ourselves will always be relational and arise from our encounters with difference. With each new difference and encounter, we develop a sense of ourselves. As groups of people and communities develop a common identity, they share a language around those similarities, and we see the emergence of a culture. But this is never a static, eternal, or natural phenomenon. Cultures and societies are always changing and shifting, many simply becoming notes in the history books or merging with other cultures. Within these societies, individuals are also navigating the norms and expectations of belonging, as well as the limits of belonging.

In this way, identity is an ongoing process, what cultural theorist Stuart Hall calls "identification." Identification is a way of describing how a person or group of people is formed by the histories and language of their society, even as they are navigating those histories in their own unique ways, either pressing against oppressive norms or assimilating to and adopting the norms, or some mixture of the two. What makes this process even more complicated is that people are not simply navigating two clearly defined cultures. These cultural realities are woven into one another, and the process of navigating communities is multifold.

This slightly theoretical framing is important as we think about relationships, because even in our relationships, we continue to negotiate our communities, our broader societies, and their histories. We can never think about relationships without also thinking about the work our bodies are doing in the world and the way our society shapes us.

In-Between Identities

Gail

Identity was complicated for me from an early age. Language was the primary struggle and tether in my in-between journey. For my immigrant parents, a mix of Korean and broken English was commonplace, and it was the primary language spoken in our house. I was protective of my parents when kids would snicker at their accent. But at the same time, I was questioned about my identity as a Korean when I never learned to speak the language fluently or practice some of its cultural traditions.

My mother did everything she could to become "American" (immigrant code for "white"). For her, that meant forsaking some of the traditional practices of her roots: she worked hard to speak as much English as possible; she fought against the patriarchy of Korean culture by trying to keep me out of the kitchen; and we never participated in the traditional New Year's bows that kids perform for their parents and grandparents because radical conversion to white colonial Christianity necessarily erases one's cultural identity and insists that we don't bow to anyone but God. (Sadly, this also meant that I missed out on a lot of New Year's money!) The loss of a particular cultural tether wasn't all bad, but it did leave me vulnerable in some ways. Add to this my slightly darker complexion and the way I looked in general, and the result was that many Koreans at my parents' church would ask them if I was adopted. I never quite fit or felt like I belonged with my people.

Later, when I hit middle school, I found myself surrounded by a diverse group of friends in Tulsa, Oklahoma, where my mother attended seminary. Not long after we settled in, I was invited to attend a prominent Pentecostal Black church with a friend from the neighborhood. And strangely, I found myself feeling at home. My parents had served in Pentecostal Korean immigrant churches back in Chicago, so there was a certain familiarity of language, tarrying, and worshiping with abandon that struck a chord with me in that church. I understood myself in that space, even though I knew I was different. Every week, I stood there on the curb of my apartment building waiting for my friend and her aunt to pick me up. We could count on a couple of the church mothers to look for us, greet us with big suffocating hugs in the lobby, and feed us after service. I felt at home there in a peculiar way.

It wasn't too long after I started high school that I realized there was something deeper I was going to discover about myself and about the racialized formation of my home that I had always known was there but had not yet directly experienced. The guys that I became interested in were mostly the guys I met from the Black Pentecostal church. While my mother generally disapproved of me dating in high school, her disapproval intensified when she saw that the guys I was interested in weren't white (read: "American"). I was pressed to either obey and stop seeing them or be sneaky and go behind her back. Let's just say, I made it work.

Our affections can often speak to where we find belonging and home—people with whom we can be our free and full selves. This isn't always the case, but it bears consideration. In any cross-cultural relationship, we need to ask the hard and honest questions of why: Why am I drawn to this person or these people? Is it the person, or is there something in the idea of what this person represents that adds to my sense of identity or lack thereof? I can't tell you how many interracial couples I've encountered over the years for whom the root of their interest in one another was a sense of wanting to prove that they were "down with brown," or an underlying exotic fetish for submissive Asian women, or the illusion that white is ideal, a prize to be won. Selah.

Brian

For me, race had always been an ambiguous but consistent presence. I am darker than my white mother, but not as dark as the other Black kids in my class. I had straight hair like my mother, but lips like my Black father. The questions of "What are you?" and the subtle glances of strangers from me to my mother and back again were a constant in my childhood. I knew I wasn't white, but I wasn't sure I was Black either.

But by the time I was in junior high and high school, my hair had curled a bit more, and I found that the color lines had been drawn more starkly. While I wasn't sure what it meant to be Black, there were others who drew those lines of difference for me. These small exclusions (a girl's parents would not allow their daughter to date a Black kid) or inclusions (being invited by the Black students' club to help organize the MLK assembly) were all asking something of me. While I may not have felt a sense of belonging, I was part of a larger story and history. My body was seen as Black, in ways that were exclusionary and supposedly dangerous or intimidating, but also in ways that tethered me to a people and a history.

These feelings of belonging and inclusion, or of distance and exclusion, were a journey for me. And the dynamics of race didn't always come out in direct ways that were easy to discern. Those dynamics have proven to be complex and have emerged in specific contexts that Gail and I have wrestled with, like where to go to church, what neighborhood to live in, or even which grocery store one of us preferred.

Gail always teases me that if we are equally distanced from two grocery stores, we will usually choose different stores. I will choose Harris Teeter with its large organic section and free cookies. Gail will choose Kroger where "the people" are. When we first discussed it, it was a seemingly innocuous detail and preference, but as I thought about it more, I was gravitating toward a familiarity and, in all honesty, toward an association that had been instilled in me growing up. Gail gravitated toward Kroger and its resonance with her strongest senses of belonging with people of color. This seemingly small detail was something we talked about, and sometimes even teased the other about. But we also had to recognize how powers of representation crept into our daily lives.

Especially for interracial couples, the process of listening and self-reflection is a necessary part of exploring how race shapes us and our daily lives, even in the smallest ways. Some friends of ours, an interracial couple with a Black, mixed woman and a white man, have a similar conversation about grocery stores, but she goes to the store in the wealthier part of town because she spent much of her childhood in poverty and now chooses stores that reflect a different reality for her.

Part of the process of learning ourselves and learning the other is beginning to question how the realities of race shaped us and them. When I first began dating Gail, I was visiting a Korean church as part of a college project. Gail seemed very different from the people I was meeting there. And while Gail was familiar with the after-church meals, the tensions between the Korean-speaking and English-speaking services, the early morning prayer meetings, and the sense of community, it was only after I began hearing parts of her story that I noticed all the women cooking instead of being in service or saw that the only leaders in the church were men.

Gail's journey in the Korean community is hers to share, but what both of our experiences point to is how the realities of race press on us, even as we navigate those realities in unique and particular ways. I couldn't assume that Gail was Korean American in the ways I had encountered in that church. I would have to allow her the space to offer and discover how she inhabited her Korean American identity.

Navigating Race

Race and ethnicity are not simply about the color of our skin or the features of our face. Race and ethnicity are about identification and finding (or struggling to find) belonging, which we sometimes resist but always have to navigate, whether explicitly or implicitly in our everyday lives.

The three particular areas that we have had to work through, and that we have seen other couples struggle to navigate, are food, church and community, and whiteness. These areas are especially prominent for interracial couples, where the currents of race and the apparent choices to be made are often on the surface of everyday life, where cultural differences or assumptions manifest more acutely.

Food

Food is the flesh of our cultural formation. We gather around food. Certain foods or flavors conjure memories of growing up, make us feel safe, and remind us of a loved one and the way we felt in their company. And because food is such an intimate part of our daily lives, and such a significant thread in the intricate tapestry of our cultural lives, food can also be a place where the different realities of race and ethnicity become apparent.

Food is connected to larger racial and ethnic realities of family gatherings, of economic means or lack of means, to ideas of extended family and friends or nuclear families. Food is family recipes and traditions and flavors of life that give us a sense of who we are. But for many couples, this was not the case. I (Brian) was shocked to hear, for example, that there were Korean women married to white men who never cooked Korean food in the house because their husbands didn't like the smell. Who cooks and what is eaten or not eaten is part of holding the racial and ethnic culture of a home. Dynamics of power and gender are at work in the liturgies of our eating. Who prepares, who cleans, whose palate is attended to, and who has to wait for special occasions or the rare trip home to receive the tastes of their childhood—these are the gates and barriers to the cultural ties that make us who we are. When we foreclose the sharing of our food and the stories of food in our lives, we also miss the opportunities to deepen our understanding of one another's racial and ethnic lives.

Gail

Growing up, I mostly ate Korean food for every meal at home, with some occasional Kentucky Fried Chicken, Little Caesars pizza, or McDonald's when we had something special. My mother would often send rice and kimchi in my lunch, or just a boiled hotdog in a bun, wrapped in foil to keep it warm. Oh, those nasty soggy buns! But mostly, we ate Korean food and shopped at the Korean grocery store that my great-aunt owned in Chicago. As I mentioned before, my mother really loved all the American things, and anytime she would be introduced to different foods, she'd try to buy some (at the "American" store) and have us taste it—like egg salad and Vienna sausages, and even liverwurst spread in a tube! But what she failed to ever buy me were the foods I saw my classmates pull out from their little lunch boxes every day. I wanted to try Chef Boyardee SpaghettiOs, and the yellow potato bread that kids had for their sandwiches, and those pink snowball-looking snacks! Most of the non-Korean food I had as a child was experienced at friends' houses or at church.

I didn't grow up eating much cheese, except on pizza and in the mac and cheese I had at other people's houses. I loved mac and cheese and pizza growing up, and didn't think much about it. It's odd how, as an adult, I'm now obsessed with cheesy meals, especially cheese on noodles or rice. As Brian has been the chef of the house in recent years, he knows to give me the cheesiest parts of the baked spaghetti or the mac and cheese or the chicken noodle casserole. But whenever I find myself in stressful situations or needing a little comfort, if Brian asks what I want for dinner, my answer is *always* "anything Korean or fried chicken." And when I've had too much fried chicken, I have to wash it down with kimchi. It's a thing.

Brian

Gail and I spent the first two months of our relationship talking on the phone and writing letters. We talked about foods we loved and where we liked to eat, but it was always abstract. When we first met, Gail visited my family for Thanksgiving. That's when our abstract conversations suddenly became concrete. We had our traditional meal, complete with turkey, stuffing, green bean casserole, and cranberry sauce that slipped out of a can and still had the ridged form of the can. And rolls. As we began eating, Gail mentioned in passing that she hadn't had butter like this before. The entire table went silent. Gail loved butter. Forget the stuffing, the turkey, the cranberry sauce. Out of all the things she experienced in her first turkey-centered Thanksgiving meal, the lasting memory was butter.

My first experiences with Korean food were a bit more tepid. I remember my first visit to Eastman and eating some 고추장 (gochujang, a red pepper paste) with rice, roasted seaweed, and kimchi in her dorm room. Her grandmother sent it. I smelled it first. Gail laughed and asked why I was smelling it. I put a little bit of the red pepper paste on the rice, wrapped it with a piece of seaweed, and took a hesitant bite. All I could taste at first was the spice, then flavors that were completely foreign to me. The kimchi was almost impossible for me to eat. I just couldn't get past the smell. The next time I visited, I wiped the kimchi on the rice and ate the kimchi juice–flavored rice.

Eventually, after months and months, I found the thicker pieces of cabbage to be a little more tolerable. Then after a few years, it was more interesting. And after still a few more years, I craved it. Part of what kept bringing me back to a food that was so strange to me was Gail's love for it. Obviously, she loved the flavors, and each dish brought back certain memories and comforts. But it was also clear in getting to know her that this food was the center of a larger communal identity and way of being. New Year's, birthdays, Friday nights—for Gail, her food was part of a way of existing and enjoying the world and one another.

If I was going to live with and love Gail, I was going to need to live with and love the food that made her who she was. It meant learning to tolerate kimchi and finding at least a few things on the menu that I could enjoy, since I also knew that

Gail (like many Koreans) would sacrifice her own pleasure if she knew I didn't like the food. She did not want to put me in positions where I felt uncomfortable or didn't like something. But she wouldn't tell me. I needed to learn to like *something* so that Gail could be free to enjoy it fully.

But to my surprise I began not only tolerating kimchi but also craving it. My favorite of all meals (besides cheeseburgers) is soondubu, a soft tofu stew. I never would have imagined loving this meal when Gail and I first met. Food may seem insignificant, but it is one of the daily stitches that bind us together, giving us opportunities to learn one another's stories and discover what the patterns and challenges of each other's lives have been.

Church and Community

Like food, the communities we become a part of, the people and groups that we commit ourselves to and allow ourselves to be seen by, are a significant aspect of our lives together. For us, this community was church. Churches were the central communities that shaped not only our spiritual lives but also our early racial and ethnic identities. These formations were not always positive, but they continued with us. And as we began to walk our lives together, it became clear that we would also need to discover how race was affecting our decisions about which communities we would be a part of, and which ones we could not.

Gail

Even though I complained at times about having to tag along with my parents to church meetings, revival services, and evening prayer meetings, I eventually came to realize how much my imagination and formation were rooted in and cultivated by those seemingly wasteful hours as a child. I remember as if it were yesterday the wailing cries of first-generation Korean immigrant women and men on their knees pleading with God for provision, healing, protection, forgiveness, and mercy for themselves and their loved ones—all at the top of their lungs. Some would be rocking back and forth, others had fists in the air, and still others would be pounding their chests. Our church was Pentecostal in tradition, so there was a lot of talking back to the preacher, and the services were just generally very participatory, engaging, and loud. Not only would I experience this in the church, but I also often heard my parents praying loudly at home in their room. Pentecostals call it "tarrying." It wasn't gentle. It wasn't nicely asking God for anything. No, it was a desperate cry to God, asking that God might intervene and move on their behalf. Desperate!

Little did I know that this kind of desperate expression of faith would translate into a strange familiarity at the church I ended up attending when I moved to Tulsa. It was a Black Pentecostal church—a loud "withholding nothing" church, where there were familiar sounds and similarly desperate expressions of worship. I immediately felt at home. "Oh, I *know* this!" I would often think to myself. The "amens" and "hallelujahs" in response to the preacher or in between songs would easily slip out of my mouth. I would find myself readily "caught up in the Spirit," my feet moving faster than I could keep up. Something about this place, these people, despite the stark differences of how we looked, felt like home, like family, but without the barriers of language. The familiarity of expression, joined to a freedom of language, was what I needed in that moment.

Brian

Growing up in a white neighborhood and becoming a Christian in a white church meant I had to come to terms with my blackness in ways that were often disconnected from the Black community. I didn't feel the deep sense of belonging and joy and creativity that animated Black communities. Rather, the beginning of my racial journey was reckoning with how whiteness had shaped me, realizing that I would be a perpetual outsider in predominantly white institutions. Only later would I come to find belonging in Black spaces.

Early in Gail's and my relationship, I was hesitant about all-Black churches. I was still wrestling with my sense of self, and maybe even the subtle patterns of whiteness that I knew were working in me but didn't know how to make sense of. Growing up, I always knew I wasn't white, but it would be years before I understood how whiteness had formed me. And it wasn't until I saw that formation that I could begin to grasp how it had shaped my desire to be part of certain communities, communities whose approval I sought and who I wanted to be seen by.

For me and Gail, church and neighborhood were where those conversations came to the surface. Would we go to the Full Gospel church in downtown Rochester or the community church in the suburbs? Would we live on the south side of the city or closer to campus? Sometimes our decisions were pragmatic, like choosing to live closer to where we worked. At other times we had options that required us to dig into our racial stories and ask ourselves what we were hoping for, what we were clinging to, or what we were running away from.

These intuitions or hesitations don't always work themselves out in explicit conversations. Sometimes they work themselves out slowly (part of the process of learning ourselves). But the commitment to walking with the other person means being open to stepping into new, different worlds.

For me, this began when we realized the suburban church was not a good fit. Or, to be more precise, when Gail said, "I'm not going to no dead church!" And that was that. So we started to make a home for ourselves at a vibrant, multiethnic Pentecostal church. I spent the first months trying not to stare

65

or seem out of place. But one Sunday, I found myself raising my hands. A few months later, I quietly clapped my hands and closed my eyes. During that year, I came to find that a vital and living faith was slowly being knit into me, something that I would not be able to do without, even if I couldn't name what it was. It was not a Black church, but it was a church that had formations in Black church traditions, where Black, Latino/a, and white folk found a sense of connection with one another and with God. That was a beginning for me. It allowed me to start seeing what my life in white communities had kept from me. It began a transformation, creating a space of common culture in our relationship.

One of the things we had in common as we first started talking was our shared experience of churches having given us a deep sense of purpose and belonging. Even as church and community shaped us, it's also true that communities are bodies of people trying to create a sense of place. Communities always have a larger history. Part of the challenge in being a couple is thinking about not only how you as individuals felt in your communities but also how those communities reflect various ways of being community and navigating a racial world, as well as how those histories shape you and how you live into them or resist them.

We have always been aware that our bodies were doing work in the world. Growing up, both of us commonly heard questions like, "Where are you *really* from?" or "What are you?" From a young age we knew that our bodies were being seen and interpreted and classified, and that people were using a calculus to try to "place" us. This was true for our encounters with white people, but it was also true in the Korean and Black communities we were a part of.

Race is not just about skin tone or facial features. It's also about belonging and being part of a community. Part of the challenge of any relationship is coming to learn and navigate the different ways belonging is expressed within these different racial and ethnic communities. For us, coming to understand how our communities navigated a world of race helped us to also see how we were navigating that world, and how those decisions and inclinations shaped our relationship and the kind of culture we were creating together for each other, our children, and the people we welcomed into our lives.

Discussion Questions

- What were the communities that shaped you?
- Where did you feel the deepest sense of belonging?
- Where did you experience moments of isolation?
- How do those feelings and experiences shape your sense of connection to community now?
- Do those communities and feelings of belonging overlap or differ for each of you?

Facing the Legacy of Whiteness

Part of becoming a couple is understanding how the other person and the communities they've been part of have navigated the work their bodies do in the world, especially in the white world they must step into each day. We should say here that while people of color may feel this tension most profoundly, white couples who we have walked with have also had to navigate newly realized histories of white supremacy or racism, which can create tension within the couple or the broader family. It is not an easy thing to begin to see the world and yourself in a new way.

It's also important to examine the ways the other person and their community have navigated white spaces. Did we come from communities of protest? Did we come from communities that valued assimilation and not making waves? Did our communities ignore the realities of race and injustice in hopes of inclusion in the dominant culture? Did our communities value some combination of these approaches, depending on the issue?

On a more nuclear level, as we grew together and navigated multiple moves and new church communities, and as we had children and began to cultivate a family culture, we had no models of what an interracial couple looked like. We were young and didn't know ourselves. We were too busy trying to survive to think carefully about each step.

But we found along the way that our story wasn't uncommon. There were young men and women in our communities who also felt a bit out of place, in between, or unseen. There were people who were going to school in predominantly white spaces and struggling to make it through. Like we've said, we had no idea what we were doing. All we had was our life and our little apartment. So we invited people in. This might not seem terribly subversive given the violence and terror of white supremacy in the United States. But we were in our young twenties, two kids, and no means. We were not yet in a time of mass protest. All we had was our home.

And in that home, people found people who were wrestling with similar questions, even if they came from different backgrounds. We did not have to speak of being followed in stores, or questioned about our grades, or asked if we "really went to Duke." Those were understood. But in this space, people were also free to be.

The last few years have made clear that racial violence is not a thing of the past. White supremacy and privilege are still present and powerful. Race is not simply about the differences of body or culture or language. Race is an idea that came from somewhere and continues to be reproduced through social systems. It shapes our communities and how we see ourselves, what we see in ourselves and in one another, and what we hope for. These realities do not evaporate when we join ourselves to another, so we have to attend to how race shapes us and our relationships.

It is impossible to talk about the realities of race in a marriage without noting how whiteness shapes communities and the individuals within them. And this is true of everyone. This will look drastically different for every person, regardless of whether they are married to someone of the same race or ethnicity or not. Perhaps one person grew up in a Black church tradition that was always engaged in politics, supporting marches and preaching social justice from the pulpit, while the other person grew up in a Black church that emphasized "middle-class values" and respectability in order to "get a seat at the table." While each person is drawn to the other, they were also formed in ways that shaped how they navigated the world of whiteness, whether in public spaces or at work.

Over and over again these tensions crop up in unexpected ways. "Do we have to go to your company's holiday party again?" "What neighborhood should we live in?" "Are you sure you're going to wear that to the store?" These questions are like a pebble in our shoe: a small irritating discomfort—or they can be like thorns: visceral and ever-present in an era of police violence and racist political machinations. "Why does everything have to be about race?" "If we just work hard, people will see that we deserve the job." "They keep asking me to be the racial-awareness guy." And so on.

Underneath all of these tensions is the ubiquity and unrelenting weight of whiteness in our everyday world. We should be clear here that when we speak of whiteness, we are speaking partially of racial characteristics, and more precisely of the ways that physical characteristics of whiteness are seen as beautiful, intelligent, competent, sympathetic, trustworthy. But we are also speaking of the ways whiteness occupies the world. Whiteness has always been about control and certainty. And part of its power is that the control and certainty it tries to maintain is always hidden. It is not like the power of the sun beating down on us in the summer. No, the power that whiteness tries to produce is more like Earth's gravity, the invisible field of energy that's generated by its mass and causes all things to be drawn toward it. Whiteness cannot be easily seen, but its presence can be felt in our schools, our neighborhoods, our media, our interactions, and even when we look at ourselves. To be born in America is to have to navigate the realities of whiteness.

Race itself is a creation of the white imagination. Non-European peoples did not run around calling themselves "Black" or "Asian" or "Latino." These classifications arose from white colonial imaginations, from the ways that slave traders counted, from how European scientists classified, and from how politicians legislated the people deemed not white throughout the world. In the United States, whiteness was a way of determining citizenship and who belonged and who didn't.

Under the specter of whiteness, Black communities, Indigenous communities, and non-European immigrant communities had to constantly negotiate what to let go of and what to keep in order to be recognized in a society with norms of whiteness (and patriarchy). For some communities, this looked like assimilation and approximating white "normalcy." For others, it meant holding onto traditions and forming new generations in the ways of their elders to allow them to be rooted. At times it has been some combination of these that has ebbed and flowed, pinned together and reconsidered as each new wave of progress or violence moved in, then out.

Whiteness is the presumption to classify, or to turn a lament about a Black man being shot by a police officer into a debate about how all lives should matter. Whiteness is sudden panic when one's whiteness becomes visible and is named and when one's only response is with tears or guilt that a person of color must somehow absolve. It is the everyday questioning or fear of anything or anyone who somehow does not seem to fit or threatens the perceived normalcy of a neighborhood or institution or way of doing things. Whiteness maintains the power of invisibility by cultivating the hypervisibility of blackness. Put differently, whiteness shapes itself through an inherent anti-blackness. And this phenomenon, it is important to say, is not simply an exercise of white people. In a society where whiteness is associated with citizenship and competency and success, anti-blackness is the way to approximate that ideal, and it can be embodied by all people, regardless of skin color.

When two people join their lives, they have to navigate this world together. For Black, brown, and immigrant communities, finding a way through this world of whiteness and anti-blackness might mean an emphasis on maintaining culturally homogenous communities to support and retreat to. For some, it might mean engaging in everyday or public activism, where the focus is on disrupting the circuits of whiteness in one's job or neighborhood. For others, it might mean choosing the paths of least resistance and keeping one's head down, doing what's asked in order to achieve the American Dream.

These tensions have been most pronounced in the interracial couples we have walked with over the years. A common conversation goes something like this: A Black man, Tyson, and his white wife, Melissa, come to us as they are trying to discern a move to a different job. Tyson is working in a company with a diverse staff led by a person of color. He's seen and has been growing in his sense of racial awareness and sense of self. But they're about to have a baby, and his job is only part time. Melissa works for an emerging tech company, which happens to have an open position that could be a good fit for Tyson. The problem is that the company is predominantly white and has little racial awareness. Of course, they hope Tyson can help them change that. He's hesitant. But she reminds us that she has been working full time and carrying the bulk of the financial burden for their family. "As long as he is doing the work he is capable of, does it really matter *where* he does it? Sure, diversity is ideal, but I just don't understand why my sacrifice isn't being seen in this conversation."

In that conversation, it's clear that Melissa has read a few books about race. She's married to a Black man, so she obviously isn't racist, and she's begun to experience the looks on the street. But she also sees the people at her company as people like her. She trusts their intentions the way she trusts her own intentions. Anything that a person might say or do isn't malice or racism, but they are just learning, in the same way she is learning.

But Tyson, a Black man raised in a predominantly white suburb, has begun to discover the depths of his blackness and the histories of Black protest and social critique. He has had enough experiences with well-meaning white folk that he does not completely trust intention anymore and is becoming less sure that predominantly white spaces are safe until proven otherwise. This divergence has created a tension for the couple; what was so certain for Melissa has become a hesitation for Tyson. And the more they talk, the clearer it is that Melissa doesn't understand Tyson's experience in the world.

Couples like Tyson and Melissa are complicated because the questions they're wrestling with are never simply about race; they're also about gender, who's making the sacrifices, and who's following whom. But it's important to begin to see how the dynamics of race and gender (or ability or sexuality) are present in a given relationship over time. It's never about one moment in particular but about wider patterns and how each person is coming to a deeper understanding of the histories, challenges, and power of realities that are different from their own.

The tensions that whiteness creates are always lurking in relationships. Whether in the idealization of beauty or in the ways "safety" or a "good education" are so often associated with particular neighborhoods or people. Some non-white communities might try to approximate these standards or find some sort of access to their benefits. Others might try to create enclaves of pride and isolation, while still others will actively work to overturn systems of oppression and exclusion. Individuals also mirror these tendencies, and in the midst of it all, they must navigate a racial world that whiteness has created.

This is true even for white people who might be reading this. We have seen white students and churchgoers begin to apprehend the history of white violence in their schools or neighborhoods. We have watched the pain that emerges when one person comes to recognize these histories while their partner still wonders what the big deal is.

Whether couples are from the same race or ethnicity or are interracial, we live in a world marked by race. To begin to account for race in your relationship is to also ask how you as a couple will learn, support one another, and grow together as you navigate a world shaped by racism and white supremacy.

These issues become especially prevalent when raising children. The choices before us, and sometimes the choices that are made for us, seem to multiply when we see the ways our children's bodies are read or overlooked or feared, such as when we have to advocate for them to get the resources they need in school, or when the teacher is constantly giving them detention for behavior that other kids (read: white kids) are allowed to get away with. Part of navigating race in a relationship is also exploring how each person is inclined to identify and navigate those challenges. Here are some examples:

- "Keep your head down and ignore them."
- "This is your history."
- "You are beautiful."
- "We need to find a new school."

- "We need to meet with the teacher."
- "Who's his momma?!" (just kidding)

Facing the reality of whiteness in the world is also beginning to account for the ways we have tried to protect ourselves or blend in, or ways we have unwittingly supported the illusions of white supremacy.

Discussion Questions

- What are some ways you have navigated the realities of white supremacy? Maybe through fight or flight? By finding "your people"?
- How do your strategies overlap with or diverge from your partner's strategies?
- What are your conversations about navigating a racial world like? Is there tension? Difficulty understanding? Similarities?

Race and the Interracial "Dream"

To wrap up this chapter, let's talk a bit about interracial marriage. In many ways, it is a sign of how the realities of racism can be challenged and the walls of difference broken down. This is no small thing. But according to the Pew Research Center, only 17 percent of marriages in 2017 were interracial (fifty years after *Loving v. Virginia*).[1] Why is this number not higher? The history runs deep. Each interracial relationship brings with it a unique nest of histories and family dynamics and ways of trying to find a way in a racial world.

But it is also important to note that interracial marriages are not a panacea. They are not a sign of having arrived at a post-racial, kumbaya-singing community. Even while the per-centage of interracial marriages continues to increase, who is marrying whom is a stark reminder that the realities of white-ness continue to linger. The rates of intermarriage are highest for Asian American women and Hispanic people. Both of these groups are most likely to marry a white person.

These statistics don't capture the intimacy, love, and mutual support each person finds in the other. Each interracial rela-tionship has a reason for existing that is personal and unique. But we are also creatures of a racial world. And what we love, what we find beautiful, what we find most comfortable is never disconnected from patterns of race in the world. We have to ask questions like these: Why are Black men twice as likely as Black women to marry outside their race? Why do Asian American men intermarry at drastically lower rates than Asian American women? How do standards of beauty rooted in whiteness shape people's desires?

It would be easy to overlook these questions, these lingering realities, and to cling to the idea that your interracial marriage is a sign of reconciliation and getting past race. But in truth we all carry biases and blind spots, even into our relationships. We carry tendencies in how we trust or attend to white people in our midst. We may carry histories of immigrant belonging or exclusion. These may not have race as the explicit label. They often take the form of conversations about neighborhoods or schools, friends, communities, or vacation spots. Race can sit under the surface of what we'd rather not do or where we'd rather not go. But it is always there.

Part of what connected the two of us, even with our very different stories, was a sense of in-betweenness. We were always creating a culture out of the pieces and strands of our lives, the people we met, the communities we were a part of. But very rarely did we ever feel like there was a home for us. It would have been easy to say that was the goal, to create a new space of belonging. But this space was always connected to the world. When we walked out of our door in the morning, it was there to meet us. And whether we liked it or not, we carried it with us when we came home. Our bodies were doing work in the world.

Brian

I didn't grow up in a Black community, but my body was read as Black, as brown. In some cases, this meant suspicion or danger. But it also meant recognition and belonging. When I was a teaching assistant at Duke I had to take seriously the fact that I was the only Black TA serving in a class. And when I began my work as a professor, I was the only Black professor most of my students would ever have. My body was doing work in the world, and I was connected to those histories and those realities. For my sake, for my children's sake, I could not pretend I was not a part of that long and beautiful story of Black life in the United States.

This meant beginning to learn my own history, pursuing communities that would help me to understand my history, and my particular place in that constellation of Black life. Part of this was also learning the story of colorism and the ways light-skinned Black bodies were so often privileged for their approximation of white beauty or intelligence. It meant beginning to recognize the small gaps my sometimes racial ambiguity created in encounters with police or teachers or strangers.

While I was discovering my own story, I was also being introduced to Korean American immigrant life, the Asian American experience, and the way Gail lived in between these stories. I had to begin to understand the tensions families held as language or long-held traditions seemed to fall away in their children or their children's children. I had to learn the differences in the stories of Vietnamese, Chinese, and Japanese immigrants.

And I needed to learn why Gail's relationship to her Korean identity and the Korean community was complicated, including why she refused to speak Korean in Korean restaurants and didn't respond to the two Korean people commenting (in Korean) about her being with a Black man, even though she could understand what they were saying. I had to learn that she didn't say "I love you" very often but that when she asked me if I had eaten already, what she meant was "I love you."

Over time, we each began to learn more about the histories and the communities of each other's people. And we began to learn and understand the ways each of us as individuals lived inside of and were formed by or resisted those histories.

Through this kind of learning, we each become part of the other's communities. In a very real way, their people are our people. In our lives together, those histories and those stories become present in our life together and in the lives of our children.

Discussion Questions

- What are the cultural or racial stories that you continue to carry with you?
- What are your partner's stories that you are beginning to learn?
- What stories do you still need to discover?

The enormity of white supremacy, its violence and power, can be overwhelming when we stare at its history too long. When we see the complexity of the problems and the ignorance of too many people, it can feel like nothing will change. And while marriage and intimate relationships don't necessarily change the world, they are signs of life. They are small sprouts of green where somehow the conditions were just right for something new to appear in the world. The decision for two people to live into one another and for one another, carrying all of the history of the world with them, is no small feat.

Part of the violence of white supremacy is the unrelenting commitment to a given normalcy, to unchanging social spheres and roles and ways of imagining life and love. And white supremacy has sought to usurp and reproduce itself through a narrow conception of marriage. But when marriage becomes a wild space of difference devoted to relationship, when two people choose to be committed to the particularity and complexity and wholeness of this one other person, the veneer of white supremacy becomes unstable, its moorings are loosened, and we begin to see it for what it is: a weak and flimsy idol.

In truth, though, the disruptive possibilities of love are not unique to marriage. Marriage is a place where the fullness of our bodied lives can be shared with another, and in that sharing we are free to be and to become. This does not mean leaving behind race and its joys or its traumas, but in this relationship a space emerges where we can lay it all down and begin to discover what it means for our lives together. Nothing is wasted.

And this is true for any place where people gather and begin to foster a commitment to discovering their own story and making space for the stories of others—a community house, a group of friends, a small group, a bike club. Any of these might also provide some semblance of liberative space for people. One way that a marriage uniquely subverts the violence of race is by resisting the intimate violence that racism exerts every day. What we mean here is that racism is ubiquitous and unrelenting, and part of its power works through its invisibility and ever-presence in everyday interactions. Racism is everything from violent police to credit ratings and mortgage lenders, from silence in response to hundreds of job applications to someone taking an extra look at your credit card.

Dr. Emilie Townes writes of this unrelenting pressure of race as a cultural production of evil. Her response is the power of "everydayness." In this everydayness, we "live our faith deeply."[2] A life of faith is never a life of certainty but a life of discovery and surprise. Sometimes what we discover causes us to repent because we see how we are complicit. Sometimes it causes us to rejoice because our curiosity brings us to see God as present in new ways. Sometimes we can only lament as we learn to see how race is violently inflicted on the lives of those around us.

In our discovery process, we begin to understand the small turns of screws and shifts in balance that perpetuate this evil. Refusing to acknowledge another's pain. Failing to go deeper to discover the larger social history that is connected to a moment in the life of your neighbor or friend. Insisting on lower taxes because *your* tax bill is too high. Voting no on redistributing funds for public education. These are always more than ideas and principles; they are everyday acts tethered to long, long histories.

When we live lives apart from another, we barely understand the impact of the everyday, believing instead that what we know about the world is everything we need to know. But part of the promise of a life together is beginning to discover the ways those very same levers, subtle turns, and questions begin to loosen the bolts of oppressive social structures. No magic bullet or simple policy will overturn white supremacy. But small communities committed to discovery, to beginning to see the lives of those who are different as somehow irrevocably tied to theirs, can begin to create spaces of life in the midst of a racist society.

Together we discover what wholeness looks like, and we garner whatever resources are available to us in order to make that possible. Sometimes this is making sure people have resources. Sometimes it is showing up at a council meeting. Sometimes it is taking care of one another's children. But inevitably these ties lead us not only to being bound with this other person but also to discovering just how deep those cords run in our communities.

In the face of a racialized world, a marriage must be able to acknowledge the legacies of race that permeate two people's lives together. But those same postures of learning—wrestling with one's own formation, creating a space of flourishing for the other, and enacting that commitment in everyday ways—are also practices that participate in the dismantling of oppression.

For us, marriage is about creating a space to discover what flourishing and wholeness might look like. But it is also about creating a space for others, inviting people into our home, to play with our kids, to eat Korean barbecue or homemade fajitas, or to simply be. In our mutual discovering, we have also created a place for people's stories of race or their struggles with whiteness (either their own or someone else's)—even though we ourselves didn't have an established path that we had followed, and didn't have any clear-cut answers. Without realizing it, we came to understand that part of what dismantles racist systems is our clinging to one another, speaking of our histories and our formations honestly, and inviting others to do the same, believing that when we step outside our four walls, we are ready to face the world, to risk, and to create more spaces of possibility wherever we are.

FOUR

It's a Man's World?

Gender and Marriage
from a Man's Perspective

imple stories have a way of being the most powerful ones. God made Adam and Eve. Adam was in charge because he was first. Eve was made to be submissive because she was second. "Look! Men can lift these rocks! I guess that means women are meant to follow." "Childbirth is 'natural' work that doesn't require the same strength or skill as hunting." "This is man's work." "A woman should be . . ." These simple stories, assumptions, and ways of seeing the world are woven into our lives, pushing or pulling us in a myriad of ways. Lillian Smith called these stories "lessons," and they were spoken over her every day as a child growing up in the South in the 1940s.[1]

But how do these stories work themselves out in our relationships as we navigate daily life together?

As Christians, one of our fundamental beliefs is that humans are imperfect, which means that our freedom and our capacity to love and create give us the freedom to act in ways that are detrimental to ourselves and to those around us. In confessing

81

this, we acknowledge our limitations, the ways we make life difficult or even fail to acknowledge that there are things we could do to make life for those in our midst a bit more whole. Confession is a way of saying that we do not know, but we want to learn. And when we learn, we want to struggle to become people who can see the fullness of God's life in ourselves and in others and in the world, and ultimately to participate in God's presence in the everyday.

Sometimes when we talk about gender (or race), especially if we are someone who benefits from social structures, it can be easy to roll our eyes and say, "Here we go again with how bad men are." And it would be easy to simply nod our heads and go on with our lives. But a life of confession, especially a life of confession that is joined with another person's life of confession, invites us to say, "My life and its flourishing are bound up with the flourishing and possibilities of the one I am with. But their life and my life are connected to these ropes and tethers of history whose strands wind themselves into our lives in ways that I may not be able to see. I want to learn to see—for their sake and for mine."

I grew up in a house filled with women. At any given time, our home included my mom, one or two of my aunts, and my grandmother. I saw firsthand the ways infidelity and alcoholism wreaked havoc for my mother. I saw her navigate the wild swings between inappropriate comments about her weight and utter invisibility when we went to clothing stores.

I sat quietly while my aunts talked about office politics and the promotions they were passed over for, even though they were more than capable of doing the work while also navigating the seemingly impossible line of demonstrating competence without seeming too "assertive." I heard veiled stories about violence and trauma and daily, unrelenting choices to be made. And I saw the ways they made lives for their children, their family, and the people they loved.

I was never the typical boy. I recoiled from locker room talk. I enjoyed long talks with my mom and wrote terrible poetry and wanted nothing more than to be in a relationship with someone. I thought I was a different kind of guy, a guy who was sensitive, a good listener, and willing to help out, hold babies, and change diapers.

But a relationship—the daily presence, the unsaid expectations, what isn't seen—uncovers the social formations that get laid brick by brick in our lives. In spite of all that I knew and had watched the women in my life experience, one simple barrier hindered me from understanding and recognizing what Gail would live with, and from seeing how my manhood worked in the world and in our house:

I am a man.

I know this sounds too obvious to have to write. But acknowledging and beginning with simple facts is the beginning of subverting the histories of patriarchy and their outworkings in our daily lives. This acknowledgment is the starting point because one of the pillars of patriarchy is that men know women better than women know themselves.

This pillar is powerful. It has a way of taking knowledge that should help us to see women differently and instead uses it to collapse women into what *we* see, and nothing more. In its worst manifestations, this gaze reduces women to vessels of sexual consumption, or domestic workers, or people whose identity revolves around reproduction. But even the more benign forms of patriarchy and misogyny distort the truth. They convince us that because we have seen one woman's experience or read this or that book, then we must understand completely—and because we understand, we must not be part of the problem. I am a good feminist. I am one of the "good" men.

As Gail and I began our life together, as I heard the stories of what happened to her at work and elsewhere, I started to see the realities of her life as a woman in this world. But it was also in the course of normal day-to-day life, in the questions and tensions about simple things like cooking and bigger things like kids and jobs, that I had to begin to wrestle with the ways that the patriarchal formations of manhood had shaped me and were working themselves out in our life together.

Invisible Work

The realities of gender have worked themselves out in our home in two distinct spaces: in our domestic life and in our professional lives. The two spaces are related to one another in some significant ways, but each has required its own conversations (and arguments) and ways of navigating toward mutual flourishing.

Gail did most of the cooking for the first fifteen years of our marriage. I would grill meat, and I could throw together some spaghetti or some other dish Gail had given me directions on how to make. Making dinner whenever Gail was busy with church was something I had no problem doing, along with changing diapers and taking care of the kids—so by most standards I was amazing! But in truth, the bar is pretty low for us men.

Things started to shift, though, on a night when I got home from teaching as Gail was getting ready to go to a meeting at church. I asked what the plan was for dinner. She looked at me and said, "Plan? I have been in meetings all week and haven't been grocery shopping, so I don't have a 'plan.'" So that night was a McDonald's night. But it began a conversation about what mutual work looked like. Up to that point, I had been willing to do anything—clean, cook, take care of the kids—but it usually included me saying to Gail, "Just tell me what to do and I will be happy to do it!" Her response was, "But creating the list is also work."

I would love to be able to say that we had a good, healthy conversation and, through our mutual sharing, came to a place of equitable distribution of familial responsibilities. But in truth, this was an argument we had been having for years, and that particular night's conversation was simply the dam bursting. I thought I was already doing a lot. As far as I was concerned, most of the guys I knew did half as much as me. I saw them reading more and writing more and going on long weekends with their bro friends while I was hanging out with our kids. But Gail was the one who felt tired and was trying to keep up with multiple appointments and cooking and house responsibilities on top of her own vocation and career. That conversation had been spinning around in our house for years, kicking up into a storm every now and again, only to settle back into old patterns.

But in the weeks after that exchange, we came to a different place. In part, it was because the demands of Gail's ministry were growing, and she just could not sustain what she was doing. But it was also because I slowly came to recognize that she wasn't thriving and there was something I could do, and that I needed to learn in order to be a better partner to her.

So Gail taught me a few of her go-to recipes, including fried rice, spaghetti, and tuna noodle casserole. I started looking up recipes for other dishes and making grocery lists. But the thing about a grocery list is that I also needed to be attentive to the whole house in a different way. Are we good on toilet paper? Is Gail going to need tampons soon? How are we on Caleb's favorite lunch snacks?

I was slowly being introduced to the "invisible work" that most women perform every day. In truth, it was a sliver of the world, but for someone who did not have to think about these things on a regular basis, it was ponderous at first. I had to think about a theology paper on the dynamics of identity and Christological history in the midst of remembering whether we had enough sugar.

When we had kids, we had begun this juggling act and had each committed to participating fully in caring for the children.

While I was in school, and then eventually when we were both in school, we handed the kids off to each other, worked in spurts, and balanced family and school life on a constant seesaw. But as I began to cook more, I found that there was a fundamental difference between being willing to do what was on a list and being the one who created the list, or even co-created the list.

I began to acknowledge the invisible work Gail had been doing every day. Before I went to bed at night, I had to think about things like what we were going to eat the next day, when I would have a window of time to go grocery shopping, and how or when I was going to make a casserole if Ezra had soccer practice and Caleb had a concert. In some ways, cooking is a minor piece within the large scale of patriarchal systems and violence. But it begins there, in the everyday, mundane realities that have to be accounted for, planned, and made. In taking on more of these responsibilities, I began to see the rhythms of the house differently.

Something else happened along the way. The more I cooked, the more I found that I actually enjoyed it—everything from the prep of dicing onions and marinating chicken to the satisfaction of people you love finding joy in something you made for them. I started looking up new recipes, experimenting with old ones, and trying new techniques. I went from cooking three nights a week to cooking four or five, and eventually to cooking every day. One night I told Gail just how satisfying I found cooking to be. And she said she was glad because she actually didn't like cooking. For her, it was satisfying to eat something someone else had made. For fifteen years, I hadn't realized she had been doing it simply because that was what was expected of her. For all of our progressive sensibilities, we had simply fallen into a social pattern of the woman cooking.

I came to see how much patriarchy had done violence to women and how my assumptions or lack of attention had limited Gail. But I also came to see how much these gendered systems had limited me. As a man, it was not assumed that I would cook or clean or stay home. And wrapped in those assumptions was a whole world of possibilities that I might have found myself gifted for but cut off from. But even more, having responsibility for cooking also allowed me to see my life more holistically, to see that my vocation was not the center of my identity, and to see ways of enjoying and serving Gail and our children that were more fulfilling than I had imagined.

But some realities of a gendered world are not as straightforward as learning to cook and grocery shop. Sometimes the possibilities of working for one another's fullness is bound up in the systemic limitations and biases of industries and communities.

Professional Hazards

"I followed you for ten years. We aren't moving." Gail said it as clearly as could be. We had been in Seattle for a few years. She was finally working at a church that fully embraced her gifts and calling as a pastor. Our kids loved Seattle. But I wanted to take "the next step" and pursue a job at a major research university. I would teach fewer classes, be able to write more, and, if I'm honest, have more prestige. In that conversation, Gail reminded me of our earlier moves, first to Durham when I went to Duke and then to Seattle for my first teaching position. In each new place she had built a life, a career. She wasn't willing to do it all over again.

In each new place, Gail had to fight to establish herself in a vocation that rarely saw women as equals. Women make up only 10 percent of all ordained clergy. And even then, those jobs are more often confined to children's or women's ministries. For all of her talent and apparent gifting, Gail had to prove herself over and over. When we got to Seattle, she had finally found a place that embraced her, where she didn't need to prove herself (as much).

And as fortunate as I was to have a tenure track position (a rare thing in higher education, especially after the financial collapse of 2008), I felt the lure of the next step, of finding my sense of wholeness in my institution. But as Gail was living into her call, I was also getting inquiries and feelers for positions around the country. The lure wasn't just an issue of individual advancement; it was also about being part of a larger system that held more possibilities for me, potentially an easier path for promotion and advancement.

These greater possibilities didn't have to do with my skills or giftings or hard work. The opportunities were available because of the realities Gail faced when we chose to have children and the paths that are closed off when kids are in the picture. We were young when we had children, but we knew we wanted our schedules to align so that one of us was always able to be with them. This was partially for financial reasons, as neither of us could imagine working a job that would require them to be in daycare and would essentially generate just enough income to cover the cost. But it was also personal, as we wanted to be present with them as much as possible. We were both flexible. We shared responsibilities. But the reality was that oftentimes it was just easier for me to work, or for me to pick up an extra part-time job. It was easier for Gail to start off part time to allow her a bit more flexibility. One little choice after another led to my working toward a doctorate and Gail finally being in a full-time position, but still she wasn't seen as a pastor. It was a dead end.

With each of these small choices and our ongoing navigation of larger economic and social realities, the opportunities available to Gail got narrower. And every time they narrowed, it became easier to justify following a job opportunity for me. We were an egalitarian, progressive couple, committed to both parents being present and each person being able to pursue their call and passions. But we didn't recognize the rip currents swirling under the surface of the water. Ten years into our marriage, we found ourselves on a strange part of the beach, not quite sure how we got so far away from what we intended.

As a man, if it was difficult for me to see what Gail was seeing in our home, it felt virtually impossible to see these deeper currents that we were swimming in. In truth, I think Gail probably saw these currents or at least felt them, and that's where some of her frustrations emerged in our arguments about who was watching the kids on Friday afternoon or about my plans to play golf with friends on Saturday. It wasn't that she wanted to keep me from enjoying myself. It was that she somehow saw how these currents were flowing with me to where I hoped to be, while she was having to drive her legs into the sand just to stay where she was, much less move forward.

Discussion Questions

- What are some moments when you've seen opportunities opening up for one person and not the other? How have you made the decision about whether to go for it or wait?

While I loved teaching at my institution, I was hoping I could write more. I would browse social media and eventually drop into that dreaded envy scroll, where everything my eyes landed on seemed to highlight colleagues and former classmates publishing articles and giving lectures. I just didn't have time for the writing I wanted to do. Summer research was actually "Camp Bantum," where I made sure the boys got up on time and did a bit of reading, instrument practice, and maybe some math before they settled in front of screens for the rest of the day. It was cooking and carpooling to soccer and orchestra, managing classes and committee work and institutional politics.

In the midst of these pushes and pulls, something odd happened: I stopped fighting. "This is my life. What does flourishing look like inside of *this* life, not some other ideal version of a life?" When I asked this question, another possibility began to slip in, and a different set of questions started to float to the surface: "Do I even want that ideal life? What makes it ideal?"

When I sat back and actually considered those questions, I began to see the moments of joy and frustration in my field, the things that I loved to do and the things I always regretted saying yes to. I started a mental list and began to see a different measure of success. The picture of an ideal was shifting. In actuality, I hated writing peer-review articles. I didn't want to write multiple scholarly tomes. What it meant to flourish started to look different.

To live a life with Gail was to begin to see the currents pulling her to a place she didn't want to go. It meant digging in my feet alongside her and each of us mooring the other, taking small steps toward a place we were not sure existed. And in that refusal to allow ourselves to be carried away by these seemingly natural forces, I could also see how the current's promise of success and fullness was not what I actually wanted for myself or my family.

In stopping, slowing down, and allowing the contingencies of life to become starting points for how I define flourishing, I was able to see new outlines of a "successful" life. Success is my spouse being able to enjoy and pursue her job without feeling like she is holding me back. Success is my kids knowing I will be home and finding joy in the small presences. And a successful life was actually possible at this little institution because what I had written and how I was teaching were enough. And even more than that, in that place, I had been opened up to a new way of thinking about my gifts and passions and call, apart from the assumptions of my guild or higher education. The contingency of my life had shown me what freedom and wholeness might look like.

Our limited view of what "success" looks like is one of the most profound lies of patriarchal societies. It drags men down even as it crushes women. It can carry us to places that we are not always sure we want to go to. But position Y or promotion Z is the ideal because maleness has become collapsed into vocation and possession. The fullness and success of our life couldn't possibly mean being in a middle management position that allows us to be home when our kids return from school. Fullness couldn't possibly mean working as a stay-at-home dad who keeps things running so his spouse can go to school and pursue their passion, or simply have an opportunity to work a job that can sustain the whole family.

The lie of patriarchy is that somehow our lives are oriented toward freedom and possession and self-determination. And as we scratch and claw for this ideal, we end up overlooking and diminishing the very contingencies that make a full life possible. Doing laundry, caring for an aging parent, dog sitting for a friend, taking a meal to a neighbor who broke their leg—these are not the seemingly heroic gestures of blockbuster movies that shape our male imaginations. But they are the salt of life, the small moments that help us see the people in our midst and learn to savor, struggle with, and recognize our own needs and possibilities as humans.

Subverting patriarchy sometimes happens through grand court cases or marches. But more often, it happens through digging our feet into the sand next to people we admire or love or simply find ourselves in community with and then struggling, step-by-step, toward a world they hope to realize. And along the way we might find that that world has promise for us as well.

Pocket Ministries

The possibility of subverting patriarchy in the world and in our relationships is no better imaged than in the person of Joseph, the husband of Mary, mother of Jesus. In Eastern Orthodox icons, Joseph is often depicted in the corner of the image, seemingly forlorn, sitting without a purpose while Mary lies in the middle of the image, with Jesus next to her. In some images Joseph is being harassed by a serpent or demon whispering doubts.

"Maybe it was a mistake?"

"Maybe it wasn't an angel?"

"What am I doing?"

Can we blame him? He was just minding his own business, making an honest living, following the law. He loved his God and could look forward to marriage, children, a simple life.

But then he gets the news: his soon-to-be-wife is pregnant. He knows it's not his. He's not cruel, but he also knows the law. He's responsible for his purity, for the honor of his name and his family's name. So he commits to divorce her quietly—no scandal. No need to make it worse for her. Her life is going to be hard enough as it is, with a child born out of wedlock and no hope of getting married.

And then he dreams. *She's with child. It's of God. Marry her. Name him Jesus.* He wakes up, and he obeys.

Matthew doesn't record a response. Joseph just listens. That's not the first time he'll have a conversation with an angel—and it's not the first time we see him with no words. Although Matthew does not give us Joseph's words, we can see that something powerful is happening in this moment. Even in Jesus's conception, something is being transformed.

While we might read Joseph's lack of words as strong, silent obedience, we can also see them as a reversal of sorts. In the second creation account (Gen. 2:4–25), it is Adam who speaks and who is encountered by God and shown around the garden. Eve is drawn from Adam's side and speaks no words until her encounter with the serpent.

Sadly, reading the creation of humanity through this story instead of through the first creation account (Gen. 1:1–2:3), where God makes "them" in "our" image, male and female, has been taken to mean that somehow men have priority over women. It has been interpreted to mean that a penis gives men privilege and power, that somehow being the "first" makes us closer to God—even though we were the first thing God said was not good. It is not that this first creature wasn't loved or beautiful. But we might say that this first creature was not truly imaging God while it was alone. To be like God is to be with another who can choose and who can love and create along with us. This is not to simply say these first creatures are symbols of marriage. They are signs of just how fundamental relationship (of all kinds) is to who we are.

But in the incarnation, the patterns of patriarchy are being subverted. Mary is the first encountered, the first breathed into—made alive through the Spirit, implanted with a new way of being and living in the world. In the conception, God is making present redemption and making plain the possibilities of being created in the image of God. Women are not just hearers, apple givers, or children's workers, nor are they secondary in their needs or capacities. Mary is our first preacher, our first priest, our first taste of what it means to be made in the image of God in the first place. And God essentially says to Joseph, "You need her, and she needs you—you are bone of bone and flesh of flesh."

This new birth is going to leave Joseph transformed, pregnant now with a new way of being in the world because now Joseph's life is no longer the center of the mission. Mary's mission is Joseph's mission. In the patriarchal system of first-century Judaism, Joseph is the head; in this new family, his maleness and his vocation are something new. Mary is the breadwinner. Her career and calling is the family business.

In the face of this new life, Joseph has no words—he has no deep insight into Scripture, no cultural analysis, no prophetic insight into the significance of the moment. What does he have? He has a name and a donkey. But without these, God's hope is dead. Without his name, Mary remains destitute. Without a donkey, they remain in harm's way as Herod seeks to kill every firstborn child.

Men have been sold a hope that is dehumanizing—the notion that somehow, we get to be in control of our own lives. Sometimes we don't know the power of what we already have, of the stories and gifts we wield. I'm sure if anyone had asked Joseph whether he thought of himself as a powerful man, he would have said no. And it's true that when compared to governors or rabbis, to the rich men in the village, to boat owners, to soldiers, Joseph probably was not seen as the strongest or wisest or most learned. But this doesn't mean he has nothing to give in that moment. Matthew speaks, for example, of Joseph's respect for the law and his obedience—attributes that are amplified by the social system in a patriarchal society. Even a man like Joseph, with what little power he has, can decide whether to jeopardize his name by associating with a pregnant woman. He can decide how to use his limited resources, including his name. Joseph still has power.

And let's be clear: Joseph's power was not just in his character or in his resources but was provided by the very social system that put Mary in such grave danger. It was not an extravagant power; it was ordinary—as ordinary as the pockets of your pants.

It started off innocently enough. Gail and I were out for a walk and she asked me to put her phone in my pocket. Of course. But out of curiosity, I wondered, why could she not put it in her own pocket? Because they weren't big enough, she said. Huh? They looked like mine, from what I could tell. But then she explained: her pockets were just for show. *What?*

Come to find out, even something as simple and ordinary as a pocket has a history. In this history, women did not need pockets because pockets were where money and other important items were kept. And more often than not, women weren't in charge of their own money. (Virginia Woolf once talked about what the world would be like if each woman had a room of her own—not just pockets.) They didn't need pockets because their clothes were not about use but about image, about projecting an image of femininity, while men's pants were about utility and carrying the means of consumption and production.

Such a simple thing. As followers of Christ, we have to recognize the nature of power in our context. Power isn't really about what you get to do. Real power lies in the things you never have to think about. I can walk at night simply because I want to. I don't have to call a friend and keep her on the line until I get to my car. I don't have to have pepper spray attached to my keys. I don't have to ask myself if these pants are too tight or if people will take me seriously if I wear a t-shirt to teach my class. When I'm in class and I press into a difficult topic, I rarely get a knucklehead who questions whether I know my field. I have pockets.

Joseph has pockets too. He has a status that can protect Mary. Yes, it might mean people whisper about him, but he'll still be able to eat. Maybe he has a little money tucked away. It was enough for the two of them, but now a baby means a bit more insecurity, and of course we know that his marriage to Mary will put him in far more than economic danger. But now, in this moment for Joseph, God is telling him that he's going to need to put his name on the line. He's going to have to bind himself to this fierce, dynamic woman of God . . . and follow her into a life of joy and fear.

We often hear that the weak will become strong and the strong will become weak, that the first will become last and the last, first. But people don't fit neatly into these categories. We are strength and weakness; we have needs and hopes that are a priority and needs and hopes that ought to wait. When God encounters us with the promise that God is with us, suddenly a light appears in our midst and we discover that what we thought was our strength is our weakness, and what we overlooked or thought was ordinary is exactly the thing God sees and says, "I can use that." How beautiful.

As Gail and I have walked together, I have often thought of Joseph and the detours his life took because of his devotion to and love for Mary. And while we don't often think of Joseph as a prophet in the mold of Isaiah or as a miraculous leader like Moses, Joseph's life points to the ways relationships can become inflection points for transformation—not only personal transformation but lives that create spaces of transformation in their midst.

Even after more than twenty years of marriage, Gail and I are still working to see how gender shapes what we imagine for ourselves and for one another. And as we have walked, I have recognized that the most fundamental act of love and devotion I can offer is a willingness to be still, to be wary of the ease with which opportunities come my way, and to be open to the possibilities that this life of contingency is not some act of valorous martyrdom but is actually for our mutual flourishing. But it will always require dissecting the gendered assumptions that float in our midst.

Discussion Questions

- What are ways a space of privilege or power might give you the freedom to go slower or take advantage of institutional bias to create space for your partner?

FIVE

Glass Bulbs and Rubber Balls

Gender and Marriage from a Woman's Perspective

aking the initial leap into a new life or major decision can be hard, but what is often even harder is living with the decision and who each person becomes in its wake. What if we have a hard time juggling everything that is expected of us and what we want for ourselves? "Flourishing" and "thriving" can be tricky terms because of their tendency to make us and others believe that our life is amazing. But when flourishing is understood as more than individual happiness, we begin to see it as a give-and-take, a pushing and pulling. It may even mean that someone has to give up something, or that something will fall through the cracks. Many of us call this impossible pursuit of balance a "juggling act."

In my two and a half decades of counseling couples, I've found that women who pursue work outside the home have to account for more of these work-life balance conversations than men generally do. Women are confronted by this impossible standard not only within themselves but also within their partnered relationships and among other women. And, depending on their upbringing or theological convictions, many women also struggle to prove their place in the world outside the confines of home. It's understandable, then, that many women feel forced to choose an all-or-nothing life path— either they can't pursue their passion and career path in order to raise the family, or they have to juggle everything and be a superwoman to prove their worth.

Instead, what might it look like to live *for* one another, redefining flourishing? I can promise you that it will not be the dual power couple and the perfect kids and the smooth upward trajectory. Flourishing means recognizing when one person has had all the opportunities, whether because of gender or privilege or something else, so maybe it all needs to slow down for that person. It means the kids might not have to be in the perfect daycare or in daycare at all. It means knowing which balls can fall, trusting that they'll bounce back, and which bulbs have to be carried with care in various seasons of life. (More on these metaphors later.)

As we continue to learn ourselves and the other, we're mindful that we live in a world where gender creates and forecloses opportunities. Flourishing and thriving is an expansive, communal idea that sometimes requires us to make difficult choices for one person to slow down so another has opportunity. Being a "we" requires us to reimagine what flourishing looks like together.

Do Gender Norms Always Win?

I remember Brian's and my first phone conversation when we were nineteen, both sitting in our dorm rooms in two different schools and different states, trying to make sense of the person on the other end of the line. "What do you see yourself doing after college, or as a career?" Brian asked.

"Uhh . . . well, I'm at this school because I want to be a conductor, but I think I'm called to ministry. My mom was a pastor," I answered.

"Really?" he said. "I didn't think women could be pastors."

He said that!

Apparently, I had forgotten about this whole conversation and blocked it out of my memory, until Brian brought it up years later. Whether I'd be a conductor or a pastor, I was certain that I would not be stuck at home, forgoing the gifts and passions I knew God had given me. I had something to offer the world. Brian, on the other hand, replied to that same question not really sure what he felt called to be or do but knowing it had something to do with teaching or ministry. So when we planned to get married the summer before our senior year of college, we decided to spend that year seeking jobs to begin my career, and he would figure things out along the way.

We moved to the Philadelphia area, where I started my first job in ministry as a part-time worship/music director. In the 1990s, very few churches would hire women full time in significant church leadership positions, much less a twenty-one-year-old Asian American woman in non-Asian contexts. It probably wasn't the best decision to move out of state for a part-time job, but I was just grateful for a job, especially that this church would hire me out of college with no experience. Brian landed a full-time job at a private Christian high school. We both also cobbled together part-time jobs as side hustles to supplement our income during those two years. It was a challenging season as newlyweds, being in a new city, with new jobs, a new community (an all-white church, which was new for me), and feeling isolated.

In our first year, when we realized these jobs were not going to fulfill us long term or offer opportunities for growth, Brian applied to a few grad schools, thinking he might want to explore ministry or teaching in an intentional way. He applied to Duke Divinity School. We were waiting and excited at the thought of a transition that could potentially allow us some forward movement and clarity in our careers. Unfortunately, Brian's application packet ended up missing some materials by the deadline that year, so we decided to keep his application on file for the next year.

Then we found out I was pregnant.

Then, nine months later, we found out he was accepted to Duke for the following year.

I realized that our baby boy was going to be seven months old when we moved to Durham that summer. The feeling I had the moment we learned Brian got accepted was suffocating. I was confronted by the thought that, in fact, gendered norms always win. But I couldn't tell Brian how I was feeling. We were going to have a beautiful baby boy! We both wanted a family. In the moment, however, I couldn't shake the thought that even though I was the one who'd had the career on lock from the beginning, as far as knowing what I wanted to do, I now found myself stuck at home with a baby, then two babies, hustling to work my part-time ministry job in those early years after the move to North Carolina. All the while, it seemed like Brian was flourishing.

Don't get me wrong, Brian was also working a couple jobs on the side to help us make ends meet financially as a family of four. During those first few years of seminary, his mother was diagnosed with cancer. She survived two years and died at age fifty-four. We experienced three miscarriages in the first five years of our marriage. Brian's situation was hardly the same as many of the divinity school students coming straight out of undergrad—able to attend to their studies full time, read every single page assigned in class, *and* have the energy to camp out for a few days on the lawn every year in hopes of getting those coveted Duke basketball tickets. But his momentum and visions of opportunity vastly differed from my experience in the years that followed.

I wonder if the notion of flourishing carries different weight in different seasons for different people. As a pastor, I've had the privilege of walking alongside many women and men over the years who are navigating this tension. Who gets to pursue their dream job, their passion project, or just move forward in this season of life? And who sacrifices (even a little) or seemingly takes a back seat to make that movement possible? Any relationship that has its foundation in "being for" the other will inevitably encounter these crossroads; truthfully, these questions and decisions will be engaged over and over again. We might as well allow these hard and honest questions to become good companions on our journey together.

No More Balancing and Juggling

I can't tell you how many times I've wrestled with the words "juggle" and "balance" as a working woman, wife, and mother. Juggle and balance. Seriously. Whether I was at the local park with other moms, or at church with other women, or offering a listening ear to congregants as a pastor, these two words have disrupted my life for years. "How are you going to juggle all of these things?" other women would ask. "You need a better work-life balance." "You can't juggle all of those things without dropping the ball somewhere. Something's gotta give!" "How do you spin so many plates in the air?"

For many women, it's not uncommon to feel the burden of juggling or balancing work, home, relationships, a social life and the social engagements of our family, and the nonstop orbit of our kids' or extended family's needs, all while carrying immense guilt for not being able to do any of these things wholeheartedly. Add to this the reality that in some ethnic-cultural contexts, if your kids misbehave or look disheveled in public, this is assumed to represent the mother's lack of parenting, attention, or care. And, as if all this weren't enough, we have to fight against significant gender gaps that still exist in the workplace, like the lack of fair pay and policies around women's health, as well as cultural strongholds regarding the expectations placed on women to continually shift and adjust to major life changes.

While all of this is true and real, I also believe it's true that many of us have allowed ourselves to get sucked into the lie that balancing and juggling is a faithful way to live. If we look at nature, at creation itself, it's never a juggling act. Life is about cycles. Cycles of life and death, ebbing and flowing, hibernating and emerging, seeding and growth, day and night—otherwise known as "seasons" from Ecclesiastes 3:1: "For everything there is a season, and a time for every matter under heaven."

As I've navigated my vocational aspirations over the years alongside my children's thriving, my partner's hopes, and a constant web of discerning which challenges were mine to carry and which were societal (gender, race, age), I had to figure out analogies that were more faithful than "balancing" and "juggling." As a pastor, I felt it was important to frame people's lives in a way that made space for women to flourish and to hold their male partners accountable. What were the non-negotiables in our lives? And do these stay the same over time? What were projections or pressures placed on us, whether from within ourselves or by others? And do we even realize we're carrying these things? Have we ever proverbially dropped things, only to discover that the world didn't end? Have we ever dropped other things, only to discover tragic ramifications?

Being parents of three boys, we had many years early on when our cupboards were stacked with plastic cups, plastic plates, plastic trays, and rubber-coated silverware. Because children drop things *all the time*. But as the first two got older, it seemed like a good opportunity for us to own some adult things like glassware, mason jars, and ceramic platters. We chose ones that would be sturdy enough for when the boys wanted to use them. And yet, when the boys would cheerfully grab the champagne glasses for our New Year's sparkling cider toasts, my eyes were constantly watching as they would throw one hand in the air to shout "Happy New Year!" while holding their glass in the other. I had to sacrifice a bit of my midnight moment in order to be mindful of their joyful celebration. The analogy became clear to me: During the times when we or someone we love is holding something fragile, it takes a greater level of attention on our part in order to not let it drop. The consequences can be harsh. But at other times, we can relax because we know and trust that the plastic cup or rubber spoon will bounce back. We weren't meant to juggle it all or perform a balancing act. Some things we must give extra care and attention to because they hold some level of uncertainty and fragility in the moment—those are our glass bulbs. Some things we just have to be okay with letting drop because we know they'll bounce back—and those are our rubber balls.

When we've experienced enough ebbs and flows in life, it's much easier to look at the bigger picture and realize there are just some things we carry in different seasons of life that are more fragile than others. I've found that anything new, or things we are potentially losing, or shifts we encounter, carries a little more weight and requires intentional care, whether it's a new relationship, new job, new city, new home, new baby, or new promotion, or losing a loved one, letting go of a dream, or caring for the needs of extended family members. New situations and shifting realities present particular challenges for any person because of the nature of change and uncertainty and because of the fragility latent in pursuing success, making adjustments, or managing new circumstances. These are the glass bulbs we want to be attentive to. Many times, if we let these bulbs drop, the ramifications could potentially be devastating and carry long-lasting effects. The fragility of the glass bulbs is not merely the thing itself but is how these new or shifting realities force us to shift—our expectations, our roles, our time, our energy, and even perhaps the seeming loss or sacrifice of what we had planned. That's what makes these bulbs in various moments of our lives require greater attention than perhaps other things in that moment. Not balancing. Not juggling.

But as with all new and shifting things, new doesn't always stay new. You won't always be a newlywed. Your job won't always be challenging to navigate (for most of us) because you'll become familiar with the expectations and the tasks. Your baby will grow up and no longer need you to feed and burp him every forty-five minutes, which is what it feels like during that season. The intense grief of losing a loved one will slowly ease, and it will be possible to find your way with each new day. And other new things will emerge over time. Perhaps your increasingly seasoned marriage is no longer the thing that's fragile, requiring extra care as it did when you were first navigating life together, but maybe now your second-grade daughter just let you know she is being bullied in class. In this season, your marriage is a rubber ball and your daughter is the glass bulb.

Maybe your boss just let you know that if you don't get another book published within the year, you may not get tenured. It's in this moment that your desire to volunteer as a coach for your son's soccer team becomes a rubber ball, releasing you of guilt and allowing you to be a little more flexible (maybe forgoing being the head coach and instead being a substitute or providing snacks). So for now, in this moment, your attention can be placed on nurturing your job. Or maybe your partner, in turn, can bear the burden of some of the things you used to do for a season so that you can focus more intentionally on your work.

Maybe you decide that your second-grade daughter will not take the bus home every day and instead figure out how to rearrange your schedule so that you can leave work an hour earlier for the rest of the school year and pick her up for quality time. Glass bulb.

Or perhaps you're anticipating your fifteenth wedding anniversary this year, but you know your marriage is fragile, and it has been for a while. Instead of signing your child up for three different after-school activities that require your carpool attention or presence during the week, or instead of going to happy hour three days a week with your coworkers, you'll need to invest those hours in marriage counseling and honest times together to process and confront the reality that your marriage is shifting right in front of you. Trust me. Your child will live through it, and they may even flourish because of only having one activity to manage that school year. Rubber ball.

Life is full of constant ebbs and flows, shifts and changes, surprises and the mundane. Some things will bounce back while other things will likely crack. Wisdom is knowing the difference and allowing yourself to let some balls drop, knowing they'll bounce back.

Mutual Flourishing, Finally

After ten years in Durham, having just graduated with my MDiv and Brian with his PhD, and three sons in tow, Brian was offered a job in Seattle, an area of the country neither of us had ever been to. It was yet again a new city, new community, new job, and new schools. I had been in ministry for fourteen years prior, and I found myself again wondering what my role would be. Brian was starting his first "real" job in his forever career, and our youngest was entering kindergarten. In reality, I was experiencing burnout from the hustle of motherhood, ministry, and graduate school. I thought it might be a good chance for me to reassess what I wanted to do with my call. Knowing that it was a major life change for our kids as well, it seemed wise for me to be the tether for this first year in their transition to a new city. We realized that our children were the glass bulbs in that season. My career could wait while Brian

105

was getting settled in and the kids gained a sense of belonging in this new city.

We quickly found our new church home, and ten months later, it became my new place of employment. I grew to love the job in ways that surprised me. Within two years, I became ordained in the denomination of that church. My career was taking off, and I was growing in my role in ways I hadn't anticipated or even known that I wanted. It was the first time in my career that I felt any type of momentum and a future I could envision, with a deep love for what I was doing. Brian was hustling to make sure the kids' needs were met while I was transitioning from part time to full time to taking ordination classes to shifting into an expansive role as the church was growing. We realized that I was the glass bulb in this season—my calling, my job, my vocational movement, and the necessary attention to it. All of this was our glass bulb.

Years later, when we reached our forties, we had some major life decisions, opportunities, and uncertainties ahead of us. Brian was beginning to receive invitations to apply to more notable academic institutions, and I was receiving inquiries for whether I'd be open to taking lead or senior pastor positions around the country. Wow. But also, "Why Lord? Why now?" Remember, I had finally found my niche and felt like I was flourishing and free for the first time in my adult life.

Brian, on the other hand, was tolerating his job and struggling to find joy and a sense of fulfillment. But he had been committed to it and to us as a family. We were rooting ourselves in Seattle because he knew I was finally thriving in my vocation, our three sons were doing well, and we loved the beauty of the Pacific Northwest. Those years of uncertainty and potential upheaval were extremely challenging for me. As I finally had forward movement in my career and the kids were getting easier and older, it was painful to watch Brian endure his job day in and day out. He wasn't thriving; he was enduring. I kept reassuring myself, "But it's my turn, right? I'm the glass bulb right now, right?" But even if I were the glass bulb, when we really care for and deeply love one another, we want the other to not only survive and endure but thrive. Those years of discernment, of finding ourselves once again navigating whose turn it was to pursue furthering their career or sacrificing, weren't easy, and we didn't always engage it well.

Our anxiety was at its highest when we'd talk about who gets to do what, and when. Opportunities and inquiries seemed to be flowing into Brian's inbox and voicemail at a steady pace. "Could this be God opening doors for him?" we wondered. But something inside of me couldn't get down with any of it. Was I being a horrible and selfish partner? Perhaps. But I was okay with that. Why? Because I knew my vocational calling and movement forward was the glass bulb. I knew that our kids uprooting again was potentially a glass bulb. "We've had to follow you the last two times!" I blurted out in frustration and fear. "We moved to Durham for you to pursue *your* degrees, and we moved all the way out to Seattle for *your* job! It's *my* turn!" I was fighting to not let this bulb drop. Brian agreed, and we tried to stick to the plan that our next big move would be for me, no matter what. Those conversations weren't cute or pretty. There was a kind of callousness that had to overwhelm my heart in order to not let that bulb drop. Would our marriage take a hit? Nah. We were confident that in that season, our relationship was healthy and would bounce back because he had always believed in my call and knew deep down this was my moment.

Fast-forward four years to today. Through a series of painful and unexpected circumstances and a whole lot of patience, tears, anxiousness, faith, and surprises, we find ourselves respectively flourishing where we are today. Both of us are in places and roles that we didn't anticipate but that we are seemingly well suited for in this season of our lives. We're enjoying it for now, as we prepare to celebrate our twenty-fifth wedding anniversary in 2021, but we also know that, in time, something new will emerge that will require care once again.

Sometimes it takes us fighting for what we know are fragile realities in a given season. Women often carry the burden of negotiating the uniqueness of what we know only our bodies can do, often in seasons that seem to conflict with vocational timing and progress that men rarely have to navigate (e.g., giving birth and breastfeeding). More and more women that I know are deciding not to breastfeed but instead utilizing bottles and formula to allow their partners to have access to more areas of care during those early months of child-rearing that are not dependent on the mother's body. Every couple will have to navigate what works for them and decide what are the glass bulbs that require particular care and what are the rubber balls that will bounce back. For many women, their vocational opportunities are often continuously fragile because of the ebbs and flows of life and the very real struggle for advancement we encounter as women. But even in the midst of those realities, instead of holding a posture of "either everything drops or every plate needs to keep spinning," considering glass bulbs and rubber balls may be a more faithful way of imagining what flourishing can look like in any given moment and season.

I know this sounds risky. As women, we tend to think that if we are going to err, we should err on the side of being in control, of not letting anyone tell us that there is something that we can't do because we are women. But that's part of the lie, isn't it? That everything is possible and that we can somehow control all of the circumstances of our lives perfectly and with grace and power? The idea of glass bulbs and rubber balls is simply a realization of what's most true about being human. We are limited creatures who can only walk so far or accomplish so much in our lives. Part of what makes marriage and relationships so tricky is that in our society, too often women are the ones who have to give up or bang our head against the wall of perfection. Everyone, regardless of relationship status, has to grapple with this truth.

But in a relationship, we also have to begin to recognize that flourishing is not a single moment but the accumulation of moments. It is the whole of a life together. When we can trust the one we are with to be *for* us, we can also trust letting go of perceived perfection to find a deeper version of flourishing that makes room for all of us, even if it is a slow process of building.

Discussion Questions

- How have you experienced the pressures of juggling and balancing?
- Have you been told it's possible to juggle life well?
- What are glass bulbs in this season for you that seem fragile, or may require intentional and extra care?
- What are rubber balls that you know can and will bounce back in time if dropped?
- What does this look like for you as a couple or family?
- What might this look like for each of you individually?

SIX

Our Golden Rule

We don't do anything big until we both feel total peace in the decision.

It's a simple rule, really. When we have a major decision to make—having a baby, starting a degree, moving, taking a new job—we don't take action until each person has peace. We commit to being truthful about how we feel, and we honor one another and wherever each person is, even if one of us isn't entirely happy about it. This rule has shaped every major decision in our lives and helped us navigate hope and tension in the midst of difficult spaces.

Oftentimes, it's meant that one of us has to continue in a job that wasn't ideal, or take on a bit more work during a season, or slow down to care for the kids while the other ramps up. But because this commitment lay beneath each decision and had brought us to where we were, we could trust that a mutual sense of peace was a sign of being called to something new. And until we both felt that peace, our call remained where we were.

It would be nice to say we developed this rule through prayer or studying Quaker practices of consensus or because of the example of parents or mentors. But as we discussed earlier in the book, in so many ways we were just making this stuff up as we went along. To be honest, neither of us can quite remember where the rule came from or why it seemed to resonate with us.

The idea of peace, or maybe a better word is "resonance"—a hum that you feel when the notes ring into a chord—has marked our lives together and shaped the ways we navigate through it, trying to listen to and serve one another, and trying to live into what God has called us to be. But to get a sense of how this commitment shapes our lives, it might be helpful to start by looking at how the ideas of peace took root in each of us early on.

Brian

Not having grown up in the church, peace didn't initially have a spiritual meaning for me. My home was a place that swung from uncertainty to joy and back again. My mother was a woman who felt like sheer love, but who was also holding a life of trauma in her body. Sometimes it felt like so much of the pain she experienced was walled up inside of her, as she refused to let it pour out onto my brother and me. But of course it did. She struggled with bipolar disorder, depression, and chronic pain from multiple back surgeries that left her unable to work, which compounded her depression.

So peace was when her body wasn't hurting as badly, or when we had enough money—maybe even a little extra to order out. Peace was hosting extended family and birthday parties. But peace was always thin. I grew up like a finely tuned instrument, able to feel the shift in the barometric pressure. A deeper sigh or a door closed with a little extra frustration would send me around the house looking for something to clean, trash to be taken out, or someone who needed a hug—anything to help ease the moment. Sometimes it worked. Sometimes it didn't.

But peace also looked like drawing or writing a poem. I would spend hours doodling or writing poems. These were ways to cope, but creating something also gave me a small moment of pride that I could look at something I had made and feel it was beautiful or funny or touching in some way.

When I was sixteen, I became a Christian because I was chasing peace, in a certain way. My mother and father had been divorced since I was eight, and my father had always been a source of my mother's pain, even in their love for one another. But when I was fifteen, I came home to the news that he had been diagnosed with stage four colon cancer. He was going to move back in with us.

What I hadn't realized was that in the year or so before this, he had gotten sober, attended meetings regularly, and committed himself to Christ. He had been going to church regularly for a year. When he moved in with us, I could see something had changed in him. In the face of death, he seemed calm, at rest. I saw him reading his Bible and going to church, and in the midst of my fear and uncertainty and sadness, I started following along. I walked to Walden Books and bought my own New King James Version Bible. In those pages I saw a God who had knit us together and was with us. During that time, I also found a community of people, friends, a place where I was seen in ways I hadn't been seen elsewhere, except in my home. Peace was a sense of belonging.

But belonging was always a fleeting thing. In a couple of years, I would come to see the cracks in the church community. I was still wrestling with my racial identity and finding a sense of belonging. Then I met Gail, and peace was like a harbor. I'm not sure peace was ever a perpetual condition; rather, it felt intermittent, almost an interruption. But because I had felt it in those small moments throughout my life, felt it flood in even in the midst of profound fear and loss, I always knew it was there, sometimes close, sometimes distant.

As Gail and I talked about our stories, trying to mine where this idea of peace even came from, we both began to realize just how much our lives had been defined by struggle. We discerned peace in our midst, not because we experienced it often, but because it was so infrequent. Peace stood out. Although we felt the marginalization of others or the lack of belonging for ourselves or the uncertain circumstances in the lives of those we loved, in the midst of it all, we still saw reminders of faithfulness and the possibility of God's presence seen in the people who showed up for us or in biblical stories we heard from week to week. In quiet, persistent ways peace rang in our lives.

No Peace without Trust

We also began to discern peace because we felt the lack of it in our decisions—those moments when we resisted the small voice, or remained silent as another was mocked or treated poorly, or when we filled the discomfort with games or shopping or media. When we were twenty, we couldn't have given you a definition of what peace meant to us or the criteria we would use to figure out if we felt peace in a given moment. As we grew together, we began to sense where that peace rang true in our lives individually and together. We had to have hard conversations when one of us felt peace while the other was still wrestling.

Again and again, we've come to realize that peace was not about the problem being resolved or getting a dream job or being sure about what was going to happen. Peace was about trust that we would be with one another in the midst of it. That trust had to grow over time as our family expanded, as our decisions got more complicated and the ramifications more significant.

Looking back, it is clear to both of us that there is no peace without trust. But trust is one of those feelings that rarely comes with ease and, in truth, probably comes through repetition or mistakes, or a little of both. Whether it's through showing up on time, or washing dishes, or asking how the other person's day was, or getting up to change the baby, or setting the coffee to brew in the morning, trust gets built in the small acts of being present to one another. It happens through little touches, reminders that you're seen or known, or that we're in this together.

And sometimes trust has to fly across a gorge on nothing but thin air because some mornings we wake up and the previous day's frustration didn't dissipate. It dug up something deeper. Trust is that layer of air running under the wings telling you that this person was there for you. Yes, they got mad, but they came back. They always came back. They took a step back and asked questions. They gave you room to be frustrated and vent. Trust is that scary unknowing between the jump and the landing, after you've flung yourself off a branch that was just a little higher than you had imagined.

Peace comes when that repetition, the jump and the landing, has happened enough that even if it was a little higher or the landing was a little rough, even in the mistakes and the unknowing, you each know that the other is committed to walking in the joy or the difficulty together. Trust is the belief that in the end you are walking with someone who is most committed not to the destination but to walking together.

Gail

Searching for some semblance of being "at peace in the Spirit" was common for me growing up. In the midst of chaos, uncertainty, and drama in the house, I've always known peace as something supernatural, because it isn't anything your present circumstances can make real or tangible. Instead, peace is supernatural because it's the way we choose to draw out pockets of possibility and hope *in the midst of* these pressing spaces. When I think about having to make a major life decision at age nineteen—that moment my dad made me choose between honoring his desire that I not marry a Black man and my deep love for Brian—I can still feel the pressing space I was in. I spent the whole night mulling, praying, and considering the decision. What an impossible space to be forced into! I decided to follow my heart and conviction, going against my dad's admonition, only to discover that I would lose twenty-one years of relationship with him because of it.

Peace for me wasn't ever about avoiding conflict or loss, but it was about hoping for possibility in the midst of these things. I've always been struck by the story of Shadrach, Meshach, and Abednego in Daniel 3. As King Nebuchadnezzar demands allegiance to himself and the idols of power, those who refused would face state-sanctioned violence and murder. In response, the three men declare with conviction in verses 17–18:

> If our God whom we serve is able to deliver us from the furnace of blazing fire and out of your hand, O king, let him deliver us. *But if not*, be it known to you, O king, that we will not serve your gods and we will not worship the golden statue that you have set up. (emphasis added)

"But if not." That phrase is everything! Those two verses describe a deeply centered conviction about who God is and one's place in God's economy—a radical peace in the face of idolatry and injustice. Martin Luther King Jr., in the face of anti-Black racism and systemic injustice toward African Americans, gave an entire sermon in 1967 based on that phrase "but if not."[1]

In truth, the peace that Jesus offered throughout the Gospels was always peace *in the midst of*—peace in the midst of persecution (John 16:33), peace in the midst of a world that tells us otherwise (John 14:27), peace in the midst of the storm (Mark 4:39). And the promise of peace is that God doesn't leave us alone or forsake us in the chaos but is intimately with and for those who pursue righteousness and justice.

In elementary school, there was a boy teasing one of my Asian classmates, calling her "eggroll" and making fun of her eyes. He was ruthless. We went outside for recess, and my heart beat faster and faster as I wondered, "Should I do something about this or not?" I don't think the boy even knew I had heard him teasing her. There weren't that many of us. His words about her were words about all of us. But growing up in my family, we weren't taught to use our words to defend or stand up for ourselves, so the only way I knew how to meet the pain was to fight—to use my body.

Like a good friend does, I walked up to the boy and casually put my arm around his shoulder, pretending like I was interested in talking to him. Then as we were walking in step, I tripped him and punch-slapped him. He went to a teacher crying. I went to the principal's office feeling liberated and at peace with my actions, despite knowing that when I got home, I was going to feel the wrath of my parents on my calves with the whip of a broken fishing rod!

Fighting might seem like a weird way to "make peace," but throughout my life, peace wasn't about an absence of conflict but about the presence of equity and liberation. I never felt that there could be peace when there were people being bullied and pressed. Fannie Lou Hamer said, "Nobody's free until everybody's free."[2] Peace to me always meant more room for the underdog, not letting people get beaten down by power. To be fair, I wasn't constantly fighting, but these moments punctuated my life.

When I look back and reflect on my formation, fighting was very much a part of my family life as well. My brother struggled for place and identity at school by fighting his way through; my parents fought their way through poverty and fought to belong as immigrants; and my mother struggled as a woman called to pastoral ministry. For an immigrant family struggling to get by, it was one way we took care of things and carved some sense of space for ourselves. It wasn't ideal. In thinking back, I realize that peace was never a foregone conclusion. Sadly, I knew from a young age that there were people who didn't believe peace was an option for them, and that revelation always pricked something deep in me.

In my faith formation growing up, I remember hearing words like these: "Pray about it until you have peace." "Do you have peace in this decision?" "I don't feel peace." As a child, I was never sure what that meant, just that God can and will give a profound knowing. Over the years, whenever I've found myself in a place where I'm seeking an answer or some notion of peace in a decision, I ask a lot of introspective questions: "Is this a selfish desire? Is this impulsive? How would this affect the family or my colleagues?" But at the end of it all, peace is an immovable feeling that there is something I or we ought to do. Sometimes it just doesn't make sense, but we have to trust.

Peace for me was always connected to holiness—that we couldn't always trust what we wanted or what we thought we wanted in a given situation. We had to ask ourselves questions like, "Is this desire coming from pride? Or from fear?" Sometimes the peace was in the decision, but at other times, it felt like a promise that would come from living *into* the decision. Often, the peace that I felt or wanted to feel meant that I was going to have to do something I didn't want to do, that there was going to be a disruption.

I'm increasingly realizing that peace is the complicated marriage between what is just and what is possible, or what could be. Given the realities of sexism, racism, and homophobia, the opportunities that present themselves and our subsequent decisions about which ones to pursue are never just about how good a person is. But even in the midst of these larger systemic realities, there are people navigating their own histories and living within those systems. Being married for twenty-five years and having navigated the continual obstacles for women in ministry, Brian and I committed to making my job the priority. Over the years, however, I've found myself thinking about this notion of peace, especially in our moments of uncertainty within our respective careers. I often ask myself, "Are we feeling hopeless right now because I am holding on to something that's selfish versus what's right in this moment? What is the decision that is going to bring the most possibility for both of us? Or do we stay on principle because we say the next move is mine, and because that's what we said we were committed to?" Peace in this sense is a kind of "but if not" peace, where we look squarely at the systems and the limitations they create but always ask what can bring life and possibility for the whole.

Throughout my life, whether it was going into ministry, or going to seminary, as well as so many other things I didn't want to do, I've had to ask myself: What have I heard God ask of me, and what ultimately creates greater possibility? Obedience takes courage. For many of us, our yesses have often been labored. But the truth that I've experienced in these yesses throughout my life is that I know God will be with me, even if I don't understand it. I don't always know what God is calling me toward, but as I take that step forward—as scared as I may be—I've learned to trust that God is going to make a way. And for me, it has always happened in the midst of uncertainty. The sentiment that there's "peace in the midst of the storm" strangely resonates with me; I find peace in the midst of struggle—the harder the struggle, the deeper the peace. I wonder, is this what my Pentecostal immigrant parents were speaking of? They were "at peace," not because their circumstances were peace*ful* and without conflict but because, whatever their struggle was that day, God was their light.

Leap of Faith

Early on, we didn't really know who we were. We had a sense of calling but weren't sure what that would look like or where it would take place. And because we had little money and no financial support from family, we couldn't choose whatever we wanted. Sometimes we had to make do with whatever came along. So when the possibility of moving to go to seminary came up, or when an opportunity to take a part-time job as a worship leader arose, the idea of peace wasn't that difficult to discern. It was an easy rule to follow when it didn't seem like there were many decisions to make.

But as we got older, one kid became two, two became three, the part-time worship-leading job became a full-time job, and the master's in theology became something that led to a doctoral program. As I (Gail) was finding my voice in ministry and I (Brian) was being encouraged to think about doctoral work, we noticed that the weight got a little heavier and the roads didn't seem to run parallel to one another.

Over the years, there were more voices, more people, and more communities to account for and listen to. It became harder to be objective because we had a seemingly clearer idea of what we thought we wanted. And when there are more viable options, choosing something that isn't ideal feels like a lack. What seemed like a good plan two years ago begins to lose its luster because we realize we aren't the same people, or we're wrestling with what we thought we would be and who we actually are in a particular moment.

As we've been together, we've come to find that God doesn't always speak in the same way that God spoke early in our relationship. God speaks to us in different ways in different seasons, and every decision had a greater weight when there were more people who were part of our community and the various communities we were leading or involved in. Sometimes peace meant making decisions that made no sense but trusting one another in the process.

Brian

One of our biggest leaps happened about ten years into our marriage. We had bought our first home in Durham, North

Carolina. For the first time, we had rootedness. Gail painted every room. I made built-in bookshelves and cabinets. We made an outdoor patio and dug out every truckload of dirt and laid every stone ourselves. We loved that house.

I was still two years from graduating. Gail was about to finish her MDiv, and I was finishing my PhD. But Gail, as she does, was thinking about the "what ifs," especially what would happen after we graduated. We were starting to think and pray about how to navigate both of our callings and job prospects and cities. "Do you think we should sell the house?" Gail said.

"Babe, that's two years away," I said. "We've only been in the house for three years. We need to let it appreciate. We can just sell it when we move." But Gail had been thinking about the complications of selling a house from far away and the hassles of renting, and she was starting to get worried. I was worried about losing the investment in the house, but in reality, I was thinking, "I've got exams coming up. I have to write my dissertation. This needs to wait."

Every few months Gail would casually bring it up. This is how we tend to work toward decisions. We circle for a bit. Talk for a few minutes, offer a few thoughts. Sometimes we agree. Sometimes we don't. Then it sits again. Usually, with each conversation we find ourselves a little closer than we were before. But this was not one of those times. I didn't want to move.

After a year of short, dancing conversations, Gail woke up one April morning and immediately said, "We need to sell the house."

"Why now?"

"I can't really say." That's when I knew it was serious. I looked at Gail and saw that something in her had shifted. This wasn't about fear of the unknown, or even practical reasons for thinking about a move.

One of the benefits of living by a rule long enough is that you know what the outcomes look like, what it feels like when the

121

decision process or the discernment process was faithful, and when it wasn't. We had made enough of these decisions by that point that we could feel the resonance of peace in one another.

We could also trust one another when we felt like we didn't have peace about something. One of the things I had learned about Gail in our first ten years together was that she can feel the Spirit, and while she doesn't force it on people or on the family, there is something about what she can see in a moment that would be dumb to not listen to.

That morning, I saw it in her eyes and felt it in her spirit. God was doing something in that moment. Unfortunately, that moment was also a week before Gail's final exams and my comprehensive exams. So in the midst of school, finals, papers, field ed, multiple jobs, and being a TA, we got our house ready to sell. We cleaned walls, sold furniture, and fixed dented corners. And with three kids—ages nine, seven, and three—we got ready to keep our house immaculate for the foreseeable future.

We put the house on the market on a Friday. On Monday we had a contract. A month later the economy collapsed and the housing market cratered.

For the next year, the five of us lived in a one-thousand-square-foot townhouse, buried in boxes. But we were able to make enough off the house to be debt-free (except for student loans) for the first time in our lives. We were also unknowingly preparing for more confined houses that we would find in Seattle. And we were able to move with no strings.

We did not realize any of this in the moment. For us, peace in that moment wasn't a list of positives that outweighed the negatives, or the next step in a carefully prepared plan, or even an indescribable calm that descended upon us. Peace on that particular morning was the fruit of hundreds of conversations and experiences that allowed us to trust one another, knowing that what we were seeing or feeling in that moment was real.

Peace allowed us to listen to God's prompting in us and in one another. Peace came in the trust, not in the calculations.

Do You Trust?

Selling our house in the midst of one of the busiest, most stressful times of our lives was not easy. It wasn't life or death either. It was just one example of a process of communication, self-reflection, and trust that has marked our lives together. For every moment when I (Gail) woke up with a call and I (Brian) was ready to work it out, there were countless other moments when one of us wasn't so sure. There were times when the waiting didn't feel holy or courageous or sacrificial. Sometimes waiting meant believing something in the other person that wasn't entirely clear in the moment.

What started as a rule—"We don't do anything big until we both feel total peace in the decision"—was, in actuality, a hope. Calling it a rule suggests that there is a level of certainty about what happens when the rule isn't followed or when it is instituted after a series of mistakes or problems emerge. But our rule was born out of a belief in one another, a desire to trust one another. And that trust had to be worked at. The hope would only become a rule after lots of trial and error.

If we were to talk to our younger selves, we might point out the places where we got it right more than where we got it wrong. We could trust ourselves. We might ask ourselves to be a bit more patient with one another. But who knows what we would have been able to hear in the midst of so little money, and kids, and major decisions, and what felt like so few options? And that's so often the case, right? We never really feel like there are limitless possibilities in front of us.

For us, the golden rule was a hope, but there were some tendencies that allowed it to become something more than a slogan, something that has continued to shape us and has allowed us to choose one another while still feeling like we were both continuing to grow. For peace to be possible, we found ourselves asking some fundamental questions about ourselves and about the other person. What do we trust?

1. Do we trust the other person's ability to hear God? We both came from traditions that described Christian life in terms of call and movements of the Spirit. We both had testimonies of how we had seen God move in our lives. But where we saw that move and how we trusted it were often very different. Growing up in Pentecostal traditions, I (Gail) heard God speak through Scripture, but also as a firm and unyielding move within my spirit. Once I've heard it, there's no going back and no waiting. For me (Brian), God's call was a sounding stick tapping out in front of me, looking for solid ground and a path forward. Hearing it is painfully slow and feels like I am bumping into more wrong turns than right. It's like smelling for good air, leaning, and following. But what happens if one person hears a call clearly while the other isn't so sure? Or if there has been a call working itself slowly to the surface for weeks or months or years, but the other person hasn't felt a sense of certainty yet?

When you begin to trust, you are trusting that the other person might be hearing God too. And somehow, because you were called together, to be a "we," you trust that the call will never be about only one person hearing. The call will be clear when those moments of clarity ring together and allow you to walk into each decision having heard it for yourselves and in one another, even if it was not necessarily the timing you would have expected. Trusting one another is also trusting God, that somehow this person next to you is shaping what you hear and what you are called to be in ways that you cannot yet understand. So you allow your lives to be open to what God is saying to you, knowing that God speaks to both of you in different ways, and in her own time.

2. Do we trust that the other is being self-reflective? It's one thing to hear God. But what if the other person just doesn't like change? And what if it's not that they don't hear God; it's that they just can't hear God through their fear? Sometimes you might think you hear God, but in actuality you kind of always feel like a second fiddle, and you don't want to go somewhere feeling like the other is the main player. What if your fears are valid? Or instead, what if they are rooted in family histories or patriarchal ideas about what a man or a woman should be?

We don't always know ourselves. If this book has tried to show anything, it's that we change over time. We come to understand ourselves in new ways, and we discover old patterns are not just "how we were born" but might have something to do with how we've navigated feelings of isolation or rejection. As we grow, we also learn more about how our body works in the world.

When we need to make big decisions and find ourselves disagreeing or sensing that we are in different places, we have to trust that where we are in a moment isn't necessarily where we will be in a few weeks or months or years. And this doesn't necessarily have to do with someone changing their mind. It has to do with whether we trust one another to ask questions of ourselves and where our fear or uncertainty or hesitation is coming from.

Over time, even when one of you is in a space that is not ideal, or you are both in spaces that are not ideal, you can trust that the other person has and is doing their own work to ask questions, pray, wrestle. In the end, trust in self-reflection is trust that the other person is open to change. It is trust that as we get older and experience more, we will have a different perspective on ourselves and the world, which will shape how we face new opportunities and new challenges. You will not be the same people in five, ten, or fifteen years. But will you be people who have learned and grown in ways that allow you to see yourself and the other person more truthfully? Or will you be people who carry the pain of trying to stunt growth and wrestle time until it bends and breaks, leaving shards in your lives and in the lives of those you love?

3. **Do we trust that the other knows themselves?** While we have talked a lot about change and listening and adapting to another person, there are limits. We can't be the person the other wants us to be if we are not wired for that. This doesn't mean we don't try to accommodate a person we love or try to stretch to respect or hold or work with the other. But it does mean that there will be aspects of who we are that remain fundamentally the same, and we know it.

I (Brian) am a pretty cautious person who has a deep aversion to change. When I enter a new space my first instinct is to find a routine, cultivate some spaces of familiarity, and just sit and be "home." But I didn't always know this about myself. When we first moved from Durham and Duke University to my first job in Seattle, we were excited to have a job and to be in a beautiful city, but I was unsettled. For the first few years, I thought it was because of my institution, or the teaching load, or the city, or the fill-in-the-blank. I was constantly looking at new job postings, and Gail knew I was unsettled. I felt like I heard God "calling" me to a new job. But Gail was not so sure. As we circled around these possible jobs and the question of whether to apply, her refrain to me was constant: "How do I know you won't just be unsettled wherever we end up?"

I was convinced she didn't really understand my frustration or my professional hopes. But what she was really communicating was that she wasn't sure I really knew why I was unhappy. And she was right. But it would take years for me to realize this. Ten years later, in a dream job, with Gail in her dream job, I found myself with the same sense of unsettledness. But I had no good excuses. As I walked around my new institution and found myself gravitating to the same coffee place, the same restaurants, the same walks, I began to sense just how hard my body was pulling toward a sense of normalcy. Change made me anxious and uncertain, and when I am anxious and uncertain, I don't ask questions of myself, but I find flaws in my environment, and once I find them, my brain can't see anything else.

As I realized this, I remembered my first few years after moving from Durham. The institution and the city weren't perfect, but the biggest problem was that it was not familiar. And I didn't understand myself enough to know just how deeply that shaped how I heard God's call, how I saw myself. So when we say we need to trust that the other person knows themselves, it doesn't mean a complete knowing. But it does mean that we need to know ourselves enough to acknowledge there are things we don't know or are trying to discover. It also means that we need to trust that we know ourselves enough that when we say we are worried or uncertain, it comes from someplace that is real. We have to honor and hold the other person in the spaces they occupy, and we can't ask the other to be something they're not, to believe something they don't believe, or to be ready for something that they simply are not ready for.

When you are able to do this, you are opening yourself to the miracle and the power of the moments when the other person says they are ready, and you know just how much of a leap of faith or act of courage that yes is. You can trust that the other person is saying yes (or no) out of everything they are in that moment, given what they know about themselves and about who they hope to be.

4. Do we trust that the other wants us to flourish? In a lot of ways this is the hardest one, the trust that feels like the biggest leap of faith, because it's not always clear. Years of small moments can mean misinterpretations, unspoken frustrations, and hurts that build like a film on a window, obscuring everything.

And for this trust to work, it has to be true.

We don't always want what's best for the other. Sometimes this is because we can't separate what's best for them from what we think is best for us. Sometimes it's because what's best for them might mean something less than ideal for us. Sometimes it's because we don't really see the person we're with. We haven't become a student of their habits and small joys, talents and gifts, struggles and daily victories.

But assuming you've made commitments to each other and have already begun to wind significant aspects of your lives together, you can start by trusting that each person at least *wants to* want the best for the other person. When you trust that the other person wants the best for you and wants you to thrive and find joy, then you can begin to make space to ask what that "best" might look like in a given moment.

Without this kind of trust, there really can't be peace, and we can't trust what that person says about what they are hearing from God or the honesty with which they are working through their own questions about who they are.

Let's be clear: this trust that the other wants the best for you is different than them saying they can give you the best or be perfect in every situation. Maybe a better way to say it is that they want the best for you and want to make it a reality to the greatest extent possible for them at that moment.

This is a trust of mutuality. It binds the previous trusts together in a way that allows two people to move beyond simply negotiating trade deals or workloads. Trust that the other wants you to flourish means that you also have to open yourself and your hopes for fulfillment to others. To say that another wants you to flourish is to acknowledge that your flourishing needs this other person in some form or fashion.

When you begin to open yourselves to this, you also begin to see that what you understand to be flourishing can sometimes be surprising and different from what you first thought.

In the previous section, I (Brian) mentioned Gail's uncertainty about my unease with my job. Her question about what would really make me happy certainly had some connection to her own satisfaction and sense of rootedness in Seattle and in her job as an associate pastor. If this had been the only reason I could see for her hesitancy, it would have been sufficient. For her, as a woman, finding a church that would celebrate her gifts and make room for her to live them out was so difficult. And I was committed to supporting her in that call, even if it meant a less than ideal situation for me.

The problem was, I didn't make it very easy. I was clearly unhappy and in lots of little ways communicated that unhappiness. I didn't blame her, but how could she be happy when she knew I wasn't? Here is where this aspect of trust becomes really important. If I had believed that Gail only wanted to stay for her happiness, I have no doubt that a sense of resentment would have crept in, a quiet waiting and pining for "my turn." In our years together, Gail had shown me that she was willing to take risks, to start over, to try something new for the sake of my call or for a sense of vocation I was drawn to. Whether small things or big decisions, I saw her trust.

Throughout our relationship I have always been sure that Gail believed in me and wanted me to flourish in my calling and in my life. It wasn't simply that she wanted to stay where she was happy. She was really not sure that I would be happy or that I would flourish in a new job, for instance. So when she asked if going to another institution would really bring me peace, I had to pause, reflect, and trust that she was hearing from God too. And then I had to begin to ask myself some real questions about the moments where I had been most fulfilled in the past months and years.

As I reflected, I came to realize it wasn't the formal academic papers and settings that gave me the most life. It was teaching in churches. It was creating in new ways. The whole time, Gail had been watching and walking with me and seeing where I lit up and got excited and where I dragged my feet. I just hadn't seen it yet. But to see it, I needed to fundamentally trust that Gail wanted me to flourish.

These patterns of trust take time to cultivate. They don't emerge overnight. They begin in the everyday decisions like where to eat out, who to invest time in, where to serve together. Whether in the small things or the large things, we are always navigating different perspectives, wants, priorities. We are wired in different ways and have different histories and fears and hopes that we carry with us. Cultivating trust begins in these small moments as we ask deeper questions of why we are willing or hesitant to do something and how we sacrifice or don't sacrifice for the other person. And as we start to see where the seeds of resentment or frustration emerge, we have to be willing to ask those questions alongside each other.

Our golden rule began as something of a whim, a nice idea that we thought might last a while. But it has become something that not only guides our decisions but also has shaped how we come to decisions and how we live into them, even when things get hard or don't go as planned. And the trust that is cultivated along the way allows us to enter those hard spaces together, as a *we*.

Discussion Questions

- What is a foundational commitment that you share with your partner?
- How does that commitment inform not only the decisions that you make but also how you navigate the life that those decisions create?

SEVEN

Covenant for Community

When I (Brian) was a new Christian, hungry for a sense of purpose and eager to know how I ought to follow Jesus, a well-meaning mentor took me to a Promise Keepers conference. At the Robert F. Kennedy Memorial Stadium in Washington, DC, I was surrounded by thousands of men looking for a similar sense of direction. Speaker after speaker taught us what it meant to be a leader in the home and a "tender warrior." They called us not to abdicate our responsibility to lead our households.

These messages didn't seem to fit with the way my mother had taken care of us and raised us. But we weren't raised Christian. So maybe this was the Christian way, I thought. It would take some time to understand the history of marriage and family that Promise Keepers and similar men's movements were trying to maintain.

The history of marriage and family is long and complicated. Polygamous marriages of ancient societies, arranged marriages, economic systems, gender roles, and children—all have shaped what marriage is and what its purpose is from culture to culture. Even in the Bible, marriage is not a fixed ideal. As just one example, Jacob had to wait to marry Rebekah until he first married her older sister, Leah—and this doesn't count his concubines, all of whom bore children who would become the twelve tribes of Israel.

There was a time in the US when the family was considered the cornerstone of a community. In antebellum society, the purity of women's lives was seen as protecting the very future of Southern culture, even as enslaved people were not allowed to marry or their marriages were broken up for economic purposes. The Great Depression and the two world wars complicated the roles of men and women, with men heading off to war and women entering factories. The 1950s saw a resurgence of the nuclear family as a bastion of American identity and even national security. That vision—a vision rooted in whiteness—would eventually reach me in that stadium forty years later.

The conception of the ideal family—husband, wife, 2.5 children, nice little house, white picket fence—was an attempt to define the ideal American identity and the respective roles men and women ought to occupy. Shows like *Leave It to Beaver* and magazines like *Good Housekeeping* and *McCall's* reinforced the images of what a marriage looked like and what its purpose was.

This image was always a fantasy; it rarely looked this way in real people's lives. It was often a rigid, unyielding framework that trapped men and women in prescribed roles without regard for their unique gifts and callings. For those white bodies who could approximate the ideal, the particularities of their gifts and callings would always be snipped and folded until they were squeezed into the limited molds of masculinity and femininity that this idea of marriage tried to maintain.

But this ideal was also used to diminish the love of Black people and communities (especially single Black women) and to forbid marriage across racial lines. It stigmatized couples who could not have children and single women who didn't see themselves in the role of housewife. It was utter violence to people of the LGBTQ+ community, whose love and lives were never imagined within this "ideal" social life.

Given all this, it's worth asking, "Why bother with marriage? What does it add to the world?" It's a question we hear more often these days, especially among young people we serve in our church and classrooms. Given the high rates of divorce and the ways that many couples enjoy fruitful and full lives without marriage vows, their suspicion is warranted.

So why marriage? And what would fruitful marriage look like? How does it add anything to the world?

We still believe that marriage is a vital and powerful way of living and joining lives. Marriage isn't necessary for God to transform communities. It's not the pinnacle of human life or the cornerstone of society. But marriage is *a particular way* of participating in God's work in the world. And it's *one* important way we are all reminded that we cannot do this work without being bound to another. We have to choose one another again and again. We have to choose God again and again. We have to learn who we are and who the other is in our midst. And the flourishing that emerges in that space will make room for new people, new models, and new ways of seeing the kingdom of God, which will change over time. The possibilities of marriage are never only about the individuals who constitute the "nuclear" family or the maintenance of cultural norms.

The idea of sharing your life with someone is powerful. Someone who will be there when you get home. Someone who will wake up with you and ask, "Did you sleep well?" Someone who will cry with you or run errands with you. This idea of companionship and sharing ourselves with someone is such a fundamental aspect of human life.

But marriage is more than companionship or friendship or having a live-in partner or a sexual playmate. All of these relationships are possible without a legal agreement or a religious ceremony or covenant. When we begin to think of companionship, friendship, sex, and living life together in terms of covenant, these relationships take on a different hue and begin to make space for something unique in the world—something difficult but beautiful.

Covenant Changes Everything

Covenant is not necessarily a marriage, but a marriage is always a covenant. Some are understandably suspicious of invocations of covenant, and we understand that, especially in a world where institutions have often abused the idea of covenant, of commitment and fidelity, using these bonds as means to control and determine people. In theological terms, a covenant is more than a contract, more than a set of terms that each party must fulfill in order to be in compliance.

Covenant is a way of being in the world that says, "I choose not to be who I am without you." This rhythm of choosing, of being with and binding with, is the earliest sense of God's creative work, of God pressing God's own breath into dirt and clay to create what Phyllis Trible describes as "earth creatures," androgynous beings that bear something of God in their bodies and souls.[1] With God's breath within them, human creatures have the possibility of saying back to God, "Yes. And I choose not to be who I am without you." And they are able to say and live into the world around them, "I am like you and I need you, and you need me." This rhythm of mutuality and need is part of the first human being's likeness to God. It was not good for this creature to be alone. Without the other that is bone of bone and flesh of flesh, this creature is not like the Triune God, not fully what it was intended to be. So they each wake up one morning to see another who is like them but is not them, one who can choose and love, one whom they must struggle to learn.

This rhythm continues in the creation of Israel, a people created from two "grains" of a people. God promises them, "I will take you as my people, and I will be your God" (Exod. 6:7). It's a promise of presence, of braiding God's own life and identity into them. And in the incarnation God echoes Adam's song in Genesis 2:23: "I will be flesh of your flesh and bone of your bone" (paraphrase). I will always be God and human. You are like me. I am like you.

And threaded through all of this is love: God's desire to share God's self with us, and God's desire for us to live with God and one another.

What rings in all of these aspects of covenant is the idea of a relationship that has permanence and meaning beyond itself. Two creatures imbued with the *imago Dei* were not to mark their superiority to creation around them, but to show how deeply God and creation are interwoven with one another. These earth creatures are of the earth and *for* the earth. Israel's life is not simply for God's play or pleasure, nor is God's creation of Israel for the sake of Israel's dominance over the earth. God speaks God's name through these people, refracting something unique and particular through their life and longing and through God's faithfulness to them. In God's relationship with them, God also relates and is present to the world in ways that speak uniquely.

Any notion of covenant that only speaks to how it benefits the participants is merely a legal agreement, not a theological or Spirit-filled presence. In God's life, covenant is a way for our lives to point beyond ourselves. Marriage as covenant is the beautiful struggle to cultivate a space where God works, where each person can discover and grow into the fullness of who they are, but also where that discovery cultivates life in their vocations, in their home, in their friendships and service, in their parenting, and in their caring for parents or uncles or nieces or cousins. And it is in the very permanence of covenant that the possibilities of life emerge in unique ways in the world.

We believe covenant is an important facet of Christian marriage. In a world where every aspect of our lives is seemingly customizable—our Spotify playlists, our Netflix feeds, our social media follows—the idea of remaining connected to and in relationship with a person who doesn't meet our changing needs or tastes can feel antiquated.

And this social pressure is coupled with an increasing and well-earned distrust of institutions. Too many Christians and church communities have alienated and abused their members. Christian communities have theologized the exclusion or subjugation of women and LGBTQ+ people. Outside the Christian realm, further reasons for distrust of institutions abound. Businesses shutter offices and lay off or cut the pensions of lifelong workers. Government feels like a playground for the wealthy and well-connected. Over 60 percent of marriages end in divorce. Too many marriages are violent or dysfunctional or stiflingly pedestrian. What can be trusted? What can one devote one's life to? How are we to believe in the possibility of mutual thriving?

It makes sense to react against institutions and ways of life that reproduce so much pain, but these failures and distortions are not all that remain. Covenant has its gifts and power. While the possibility of choice is alluring, isn't it also overwhelming at times? We have access to the possibility of everything, and yet nothing seems to meet our needs. We move from job to job or from city to city, and while we discover new things in each place, the roots never have time to grow. It begins to feel easier to keep moving rather than discover the depths of a place (or a person).

A covenant relationship is one that roots us in the world with *this* person and not *that* person. This rootedness can be difficult as we try to navigate who we are and who we are becoming alongside this other person who sometimes sees us and sometimes doesn't, and who is growing in their own ways. But the rootedness can also be a gift. As we grow and work and toil, even in our mistakes and unknowing, this person tethers us, allowing us to find the water and nourishment that is deep in the ground where we have been planted together, rather than uprooting ourselves and trying to plant in new places over and over again.

Why Marriage Matters

While we are trying to hold up the possibilities and beauty of marriage, we also want you to hear it again: marriage is not the be-all and end-all. Marriage is one point in a constellation of relationships that make up our social fabric. Some of the fundamental aspects of marital relationships are present in all relationships in their own way—things like mutual respect, trust, sticking by, learning, and being transparent. Whether in friendships or in parent/child relationships or in relationships with close colleagues, these are habits and virtues that we need to cultivate in order to build deep, meaningful bonds with people.

So how is marriage different, and why does it matter? When we entered that little church twenty-some years ago, we entered as individual people. At any point before those words were uttered, we could have turned back and said, "I don't think this is the right decision." And we would have left as people who used to be engaged. One or both of us might feel bitter, or sad, or relieved about that outcome, but neither of us would be an ex-spouse.

In the legal and religious ceremony of marriage, our commitment to one another becomes public. We become an entity, a small little community that exists inside of and for the larger community. In a way, the public oath is a part of this transformation. We commit to one another and are joined by a pastor or a judge or a person recognized by an authority beyond the two of us, and we make an oath to be committed to one another, to love, to hold, to stand by, to care for.

What makes a marriage different from a friendship is the power of covenant and the legal and spiritual bonds that are formalized through a religious community and/or the state. While these bonds can be broken, they are irrevocable in the sense that these two lives, and all the lives that are connected to them, will never be the same. The intertwining of daily life, the intimacy of sexual lives, perhaps the sharing of children and finances—all of these threads weave two people together to become something different than friends. The two have become one, bone of my bone and flesh of my flesh, as Genesis states.

But part of what makes this public declaration of fidelity and devotion and care so powerful is not only what the oath means for the participants. This public commitment is also powerful because it invites accountability. This couple is not only a new body for one another; they are a new body for their community. They are inviting the community to hold them, to support them as they begin this life together. And even as the community helps to support them, they also are creating a home that will serve the community by becoming a new space of life in the midst of the community.

Just as a lawyer pledges an oath after passing the bar exam, or a doctor pledges the Hippocratic oath upon completion of their degree, the public marriage declaration is an entrance into a larger body that the couple is connected to and that is connected to them. The power of the oath lies in its capacity to transform the identities of each person. Whether with a name change or a ring, it changes us. In the same way, the dissolution of that relationship also leaves a mark on us, making us widows or *ex*-husbands or *ex*-wives. Whether there are children involved or not, there are ties that bind us to that person that are sewn and stitched into the daily intimacies of life together that do not fade away.

One way to think of covenant is like the spines of a basket, the structure of thicker sticks that thinner branches are woven through. The spine, as the structure of the basket, is not what makes it a basket. Yet without that structure the sticks are no use for carrying anything. But that structure also bends the sticks together, toward one another, allowing them to move in and out of the other branches until a space begins to form, a shape that can hold, that can carry.

The permanence of covenant, of that structure that can feel like it limits us, is also what makes space and purpose possible. In our years of marriage, it has not always been bliss. While we are flattered by the #powercouple and #relationshipgoals monikers, the truth is that we wrestled and pressed and chafed throughout the years. For everything we are proud of, there are stretch marks and scars big and small, trust that had to be healed and restored. In those moments when we weren't sure we were going to make it, when we each started to quietly do the calculus in our heads of what life would look like without the other, what brought us back was this deep sense of covenant. Not the legal sense of divorce or obligation, but covenant in the sense of, Who am I without this person? Bone of my bone and flesh of flesh: I choose not to be who I am without you.

When we do the math and try to unravel the basket, we find that our shape has bent toward the other. We are encircled, entwined with one another, and if we are honest, who we are, both in our difficulties and in our joys, was not possible without this other person. So we stay. We listen. We learn. We wait. We grow. We talk. We allow one another to be reminded of the journeys and the transformations and the kernels of who each of us was and always will be.

There is something freeing in the ways covenant ties us together. It calls us back again and again to one another. And with each return, we find our dreams to be wider than we might have imagined. Or we might find that our dreams and our hopes are already realized when we take stock of who we are and who we get to share it with. Within this spine of covenant, we also begin to find the freedom to discover, to change, to become in new ways.

A Community of Relationships

We've mentioned that both of us lacked models. In an ideal world we both would have been able to build on parents and families who formed us into ways of loving and living. And having to piece together ways of walking together in life wouldn't be the whole story. In truth, though, our life was also made possible by people who walked with us over the course of months and years. Some were newly married couples. Some were single people who found small spaces of life in our home and who came alongside us to watch kids or bring food or encourage us on our journey.

In these relationships, folks also gave us small bits of wisdom or caused us to slow down and ask questions of ourselves. The possibility of learning and growing also meant we had to risk actually revealing the truth of our life together. When we were at Duke a couple stayed with us one night a week instead of doing a long commute during the week. Most nights this was a wonderful time of cooking, hanging out, or studying with friends.

But as the weeks went on, the ordinary rhythms of life revealed the crags and rough patches that couldn't be thrown into the coat closet until guests left. Sometimes little disagreements or frustrations spilled out. On one of these nights our friends sat with us. They had only been married a few years. We had been married twice as long and had two kids. What could we possibly learn from them? But on that night, we needed them to help us hear each other, to help keep us from devolving into the usual patterns. At first, we were a little embarrassed. But as each difficult hour passed, we had to let our friends into the disagreements and hurts and disappointments, and even more difficult, we had to reveal our shortcomings as people. They stayed up with us until 4 a.m.—and after a few hours of sleep before starting a new day, we were able to keep moving, to see each other again, and to remember who we wanted to be to one another.

Single people have also poured into us in ways we can't measure. We have learned of new restaurants and hot spots in town that we would never have found on our own with our usual 4:30 p.m. dinner. (Eating out with three young kids is no small task!) But even more than social networks and babysitting, the single people in our lives helped us to remember small joys, to recognize that our little life was not ours alone and that there were realities people faced every day beyond our tiny apartment while we were just trying to get from naptime to bedtime. They connected us to a world we would have too easily driven by. One of our single friends came over for dinner after trips to India and talked to us about her work with trafficked women. Another friend organized protests after yet another killing of a Black person by police. Another would sit and tell us about the inner workings of corporate America and the challenges of being a Black woman. Our marriage needed these people and their gifts and experiences and struggles. Their lives would inform how we imagined our vocation.

This community has been especially welcome and helpful as we have raised our three boys. While each of them is similar to us in their own ways, we also realized early on that the two of us didn't have all the resources or experience or insight our kids needed. Oftentimes friends who shared similar interests with our children were able to be someone they could talk to. Sometimes it was hand-me-down audio equipment for a child who was just getting into recording.

But most often it was someone who wasn't inside of our daily, incremental, just-trying-to-get-to-naptime life who could remind us of the wonder of our children. Our kids are amazing, don't get us wrong. But we often get so caught up and fixated on the frustrations and rough patches that it is hard to see the strides, the victories, the amazing people those little children were becoming. In truth, we needed this for ourselves; we needed people in our lives to remind us that we are real people. In some cases that meant letting them see the closets and the rooms not meant for guests. And we also needed people to remind us of the wins, of just how much life was running through our little marriage.

There is no relationship that is sealed off from the world. Just as the marital relationship is a nest of stories and histories woven together, marriages are also caught up in a vast network of relationships. The relationships in this ecosystem feed and support each other, all the relationships learning and growing from how the others exist in the world. Yes, in our marriage we tried to create spaces of life and rest for people along the way. And we believe that our mutual flourishing could create a space for others in our respective vocations and in our lives with each other. But this life was also made possible by all the people we found ourselves alongside. We all fed and ate, offered and received. Our marriage would be very different without these people in our lives. Marriage is always a communal journey, for us and for those we meet along the way.

Marriage serves the community in its collective life. And it serves the community in that it allows each person to flourish wherever they are, in or out of the home. But marriage is only one of the baskets feeding the neighborhood. In the same way that ecosystems require biodiversity in order to thrive, communities also thrive when we recognize the many ways people relate and commit to one another—whether as friends or family or neighbors or colleagues. Each of these, when oriented toward the possibility of a thriving mutuality, allows all of us to grow and discover, to create and sustain small cultures of mutual thriving and flourishing.

In the permanence and daily intimacy of life together, we grow. Our roots reach deep into the soil, seeking nourishment and life, and weave into one another, allowing everything we see above the ground to bear fruit. But it is also covenant that allows us to see that our flourishing is bound up with the other. Part of the gift of a life together is that when one of us gets an amazing job opportunity, the question is also an opportunity for the other to take stock and reassess their vocation. Our lives are intertwined. And this is a gift because it means that the time when we have to wait, or the risks we both have to venture into, or the compromises one of us must inevitably make, these realities are also teaching us.

In that ebb and flow of pressing or slowing down, of having to live our life wound up in the life of this other person, we also begin to find new ways that our lives and our bodies do work in the world. While I (Brian) might have thought that working at a small liberal arts school wasn't doing much for me professionally, Gail's presence leading worship or preaching was connected to our life together. My life with Gail pressed me into new ways of inhabiting my manhood, which gave me the freedom to sit still (as best I could)—and even that sitting still speaks in the world, just like *not* following the dream job can also create in the world.

Within the spine of covenant and trust and commitment to one another's flourishing, something amazing can happen: you discover that your lives are opening up possibilities for others. In the freedom of being bone of bone and flesh of flesh, you are able to fail and grow and change, knowing that this person has committed themselves not only to who you are but to who you will become. And in that space, those who live in your home, who you work with, who you live next door to also are shaped by your life together.

Sometimes the hard part of living a life day in and day out with someone is that we miss the growth because it is too subtle. The daily grind or to-do lists begin to cover over what was once the beautiful grain of an oak table or the shine of a favorite picture. Or the frustrations of a world that seems to beat us down can still weigh on us at home, even in a place that should feel safe. So we have to fight to make the smallest bit of room for ourselves, and before we know it, the home is its own kind of competition. And because we have lost sight of the beauty of those people who are in our life or feel like we can't depend on this person to join their life to ours, we miss the small changes and transformations that are beginning or that are possible.

But a life of commitment to one another will never be the accumulation of completed plans or a predetermined picture of the perfect couple or perfect family. In truth, a flourishing marriage is measured by the degree to which each person is able to live and grow and discover their call, their passion, their whole selves because of whom they share their life with. We hold the plans lightly because we never know what comes or who we are becoming along the way. That hope and faith in the other's possibilities and in our commitment to them is the joy of a life together. The power and possibility of marriage is the gift of a relationship that makes space to fail, to enjoy, to change, to not need to be perfect, and to live into a life of learning. It all goes in the basket. It all gets used, creating opportunities to nourish and grow and cultivate life in all its varieties if both people are willing to live into the other. That's the gift and the challenge of choosing *us*.

Discussion Questions

- What does your marriage mean for your community?
- What are ways that creating a space of flourishing for your partner might also create space for others outside your home?
- Marriage isn't only about creating spaces but also learning and receiving. How do the single people in your life model love and flourishing?

Acknowledgments

Writing a book on marriage while quarantined together during a pandemic was harder than we thought and more rewarding than we could have ever imagined. This book would not have been possible without our editor, Katelyn Beaty, who believed we had something valuable to share, who walked with us as we conceived of the book, and whose thoughtful comments helped to clarify what we hoped to convey. To everyone at Brazos Press and Baker Publishing who helped with editing, copyediting, designing, marketing, and all the other details that went into making our book come to life, thank you.

We were always loved. Growing up in homes that were filled with turmoil and uncertainty, our parents did the best they could. Each of them loved us as best as they knew how. We lost them too soon, but even now, we can see small ways that their lives and legacy are present in ours.

To our three favorite humans in the world, Caleb, Ezra, and Joseph—aka Caba, Ezbo, and Junebug—you continually inspire us to live into our best and fullest selves. We pray that our lives have become small seeds of imagination and dusty trails of possibility for you in the face of all the naysayers and boundaries you will encounter along the way. But more than anything, thank you for letting us think that we were the dopest parents for as long as you did, and for already planning how you'll take us into your homes when we don't want to pay rent anymore and have no teeth. #ChoosingUs #squadBANTUM

Not having the luxury of our parents being around for us, our understanding of family evolved and expanded over the years. Part of what made it possible for us to be where we are today was a community of people who walked with us, tangibly supported us, and deeply demonstrated their love for us and our children throughout our lives together. There were countless people who were like family for our boys while we were in classes at Duke, at meetings after church, in music rehearsals at night, and away on overnight out-of-town trips when we both had speaking engagements, interviews, anniversary getaways, and those most challenging hours of labor and delivery. Our community's presence made our lives possible, giving us small moments to pursue our callings or reconnect with one another as we fumbled our way toward this life together. We especially want to thank Tanvi Mohan, Leashia Pope, Christina Williams, Amey Victoria Adkins-Jones, Carrie and Jonathan Tran, Minhee and Eugene Cho, Joanie Komura, Deanne Liu, and Roxy and Matt Hornbeck for the ways you helped care for our boys when we needed it most.

To our Regroup, for the privilege of getting to walk with you in all of your various stages of young adulthood, we say thank you. In navigating everything from singleness, to engagements, to married life, to parenthood—you were willing to be community to one another and to us. While we hosted, we also learned. Your lives are a constant source of joy and encouragement for us.

In addition to walking with younger couples, we have also learned from watching couples who are four and five steps ahead of us. While we have had the privilege of admiring many couples and partnerships from afar, we want to especially show love for Willie and Joanne Jennings, who heard us in our individual struggles over the years and showed us what choosing the other looks like in the everyday; and to Brenda Salter McNeil, whose life and love have demonstrated what friendship looks like when we choose mutual flourishing, continually breaking boundaries together.

Notes

Chapter 3: Race and Belonging

1. Gretchen Livingston and Anna Brown, "Intermarriage in the U.S. 50 Years after *Loving v. Virginia*," Pew Research Center, May 18, 2017, https://www.pewresearch.org/social-trends/2017/05/18/intermarriage-in-the-u-s-50-years-after-loving-v-virginia.

2. Emilie Townes, *Womanist Ethics and the Cultural Production of Evil* (New York: Palgrave MacMillan, 2006), 165.

Chapter 4: It's a Man's World?

1. Lillian Smith, *Killers of the Dream* (New York: Norton, 1994).

Chapter 6: Our Golden Rule

1. Martin Luther King Jr., "But, If Not," sermon, Ebenezer Baptist Church, Atlanta, Georgia, November 5, 1967, available at https://youtu.be/0-kgkeuNOB4.

2. Fannie Lou Hamer, "Nobody's Free until Everybody's Free," speech, July 10, 1971, Washington, DC, National Women's Political Caucus, in *The Speeches of Fannie Lou Hamer: To Tell It Like It Is*, ed. Maegan Parker Brooks and Davis W. Houck (Jackson: University Press of Mississippi, 2011), 134.

Chapter 7: Covenant for Community

1. Phyllis Trible, "Eve and Adam: Genesis 2–3 Reread," in *Womanspirit Rising: A Feminist Reader in Religion*, ed. Carol P. Christ and Judith Plaskow (New York: HarperOne, 1992), 74–83.